The **Red Carpet** Guide to **Sydney**

The Essential Guide to Sydney's
Celebrity Hot Spots

Renae Leith-Manos & Kristy Meudell

NEW
HOLLAND

Contents

Sydney & Surrounding Regions

4

SYDNEY
Credentials of
a Celebrity City

Star Qualities

'I love Sydney. If I ever get kicked out of America, I'm coming to live here.' **Robbie Williams, singer**

It may have been left up to Robbie Williams to make one of the greatest public declarations of love to Australia's most globally renowned city, but he isn't the only celebrity to feel this way. Though Los Angeles and London are still home to the majority of the world's most famous faces, Sydney has become their unofficial playground. Some come purely for fun, but more come to work. Film studios have made more than 229 movies in Sydney and the city has made a cameo appearance in many others. Among the films shot here are *Superman Returns, Moulin Rouge!, Mission Impossible II, Star Wars* episodes II and III, *Superman Returns, Dark City, The Matrix, Finding Nemo, Strictly Ballroom, Muriel's Wedding*, and *Dirty Deeds*.

Whether for business or pleasure, the who's who of the entertainment world have been drawn 'down under'. If Sydney had an official visitor book, it would boast more names than a red carpet awards ceremony. Within the following pages, the places that have attracted the world's biggest stars have been revealed—from hotels and restaurants to fashion boutiques and iconic attractions. Along with listings of these celeb drawcards—the hotspots where stars like to dine, stay and play—a plethora of celebrity stories connected with these places are also revealed. Many have never been disclosed until now, yet for every story told, there as just as many that remain untold—the world of celebrity is one shrouded in secrecy after all.

This guide contains enough information to create your own VIP experience in Sydney, so follow the maps and use the suggestions to create your own star studded Sydney itinerary. Who knows, as you sashay through the city feeling like a star yourself, chances are you might just run into one.

Vibe

'Sydney is incredibly beautiful. It has a great energy. I really feel at home here.' **Cindy Crawford, model**

Exciting and glamorous, spectacularly beautiful and bursting at the seams, with so many events, people, places and restaurants—welcome to Sydney. If you're not careful, a week will exhaust you, but then, that's all part of the appeal. There's sun, surf and sand, but then there's so much more. Sydney is an epicentre for everything that is happening right now—shopping, dining, nightlife, music, parties.

Sydneysiders rate as the most ambitious of Australians. Many are originally interstaters, but they all want to make it—right now. Cash, cars, designer denim, a table in a top restaurant, it's all on their list. Plus, they want to ensure they're **on** the list, the A-list invite list, that is.

It's competitive, it's fast, and it's just one reason why everything here is pricier than anywhere else in Oz. Whether it's real estate, a coffee or a kaftan, the closer you are to the hub, the more you will pay. But it's so much fun—and serious socialites worthy of their Manolos won't want to miss one second of the action.

Weather

'The weather is lovely and the people are nice. I think Sydney is fantastic.' **Jennifer Aniston, actor**

Ask any Sydneysider about the weather and they will confidently inform you that it is the best in the world. And they've got a point—nine months of the year are warm to hot, and even the winter months feature sunny days and clear skies most of the time. December to February can be humid, so request the airconditioning to be turned on!

Transport

'A lot of people commute by boat from wherever they live. So the city is a constant motion of people going from one place to the next by boat.' **Kate Bosworth, actor**

The taxi services here aren't up quite the same standard as other international locales so try and be clear with addresses and cross streets. You can usually hail a cab on the street and the Silver Service (133 300) and Black Prestige fleets are the pick of the crop. Trains are fairly reliable and cheap, and will save your Jimmy Choos, as are buses, ferries, the light rail and Jet Cats. Cars can also be hired at a relatively low cost, though parking is a nightmare and the city has extremely strict parking policies (fines start at around $75). If you're walking, don't cross without the lights and though most areas are generally safe, check which areas are safe to walk around in after dark.

Gossip & News

'I had a great time in Sydney and the people were extraordinary— although occasionally I'd read somewhere which store I'd been into and which book I'd bought.' **Keanu Reeves, actor**

The Daily Telegraph newspaper has a daily celebrity section, Sydney Confidential, full of updates and sightings, and even its own spin-off TV show, *Confidential*, which airs on Foxtel. On the weekend, their gossip guru, Ros Reines, writes tantalising bits in the back section of *The Sunday Telegraph*. *The Sun-Herald* also has a well-read social section called 'S'. *Woman's Day* is the most read weekly gossip mag, with *New Idea* not far behind, while *The Australian Women's Weekly* is a monthly full of interviews and stories with Australian celebs. Monday to Friday, 2DayFM radio's 'Breakfast Show' is also a great place to be informed with the latest happenings in the celebrity world.

Wining & Dining

'*When I'm not in Sydney I miss the wine and food so much.*'
Sarah Wynter, actor

Eating out has become a status symbol in Sydney, and chefs are celebrities in their own right. They have their own cookbooks, newspaper columns, cookware ranges and permanent place in the gossip pages. Sydney is where Neil Perry, Tetsuya Wakuda, Christine Manfield and many others were thrust into superstardom, so if it's A-list dining you're after, be sure to book. When they're hot, the top restaurants are on fire and waiting lists for Friday and Saturday nights and weekend lunches can be up to six weeks long.

Similarly with bars and clubs, door lists and memberships are common practice at the hottest spots. Drinking is legal for those aged 18 and over, but smoking is now prohibited by law in all enclosed public spaces—including restaurants, bars and pubs and at beaches including Manly, Bondi and Tamarama. There are hefty fines for anyone caught smoking in smoke-free areas.

Sport

'*Whenever I'm not living here, it's like "what am I doing?" I miss it when I'm not here. And I also miss the little things like the footy and eating pies and Paddlepops.*' Simon Baker, actor

Sport is a national pastime, and Sydneysiders are especially passionate about their cricket, tennis, rugby league, rugby union and horseracing. Sydney is the headquarters of the Australian Rugby League with nine of the 16 National Rugby League (NRL) teams based here. The South Sydney Rabbitohs—who were bought by a group of businessmen including Russell Crowe in 2007—are the team to watch for celebrity fans. Sydney has teams in most other national sports, and at the time of going to press, actor Anthony La Paglia who is a shareholder in Sydney FC (a soccer team in the domestic A-league) and Russell Crowe were in talks to build a 25,000 seat stadium that each of their teams could use.

Music

'I've noticed that a lot of the venues that did close down are back... Maybe it's the nature of the city reasserting itself. Sure it's not the same as the '70s, but...the quality of the music is more consistent. There's also greater variety.' **Tim Freedman, The Whitlams**

Australian groups and artists originating in Sydney include AC/DC, Rose Tattoo, Midnight Oil, INXS, Noiseworks, Hoodoo Gurus, The Church, Radio Birdman, You Am I, The Cruel Sea, The Whitlams, Alex Lloyd, and Wolfmother. However, the Australian live music scene has suffered over the last few years due to the introduction of poker machines into the traditional haven of live music—the great Aussie pub. Thankfully there are still some great venues in which to check out some live acts, particularly in the city's inner west.

Dress Code

'Australian designers tend to have a lot of very colourful, pretty and unique designs. A lot of the labels do beautiful sun dresses and quirky girly things.' **Mischa Barton, actor**

When it comes to daywear in Sydney, anything goes, that is so long as it's a mix of sexy, glam and smart. Havaianas (rubber thongs for your feet) can be worn just about everywhere. Friday is usually casual day in all but the most conservative city offices and if there's a crazy fashion trend going on, you'll see it in Sydney.

At night, even in the best restaurants, people are casual compared to international standards—it's a type of Sydney statement. Designer brands, premium and streetwear, are held in high regard, but as long as you step out with confidence and a dash of attitude, you'll be fine.

Paparazzi

'*We did the premiere for* The Fast and the Furious *in Sydney and it was bigger than the one we had back home in the States as far as the turnout outside the cinema was concerned—the paparazzi and the fans. I was blown away.*' **Paul Walker, actor**

The paparazzi are always lurking around Sydney waiting for a celebrity to pop up. They've been labelled as vicious, threatening and invasive, but that doesn't seem to put them off the trail. Nicole Kidman, Hugh Jackman and Russell Crowe are regular targets, but with the large number of visiting celebs, these tireless snappers are on the case every day. Regular places you can see them are Woolloomooloo wharf, and anywhere near the harbour.

Contactability

'*It's a long trek and you can't exactly just come for the weekend...*'
Sarah Wynter, actor

Australia is just a phone call away to anywhere in the world. The country code is **+61**, and **2** is the code for Sydney. All the phone numbers in this book have (02) as a prefix. Dial (02) only when you are calling outside the state of NSW. In an emergency, call **000**. And Sydneysiders call cell phones, mobiles.

Celebrity Shortlist

Social Events

'The Sydney Gay and Lesbian Mardi Gras is one of the big showstoppers of the year. There's a scene in Romeo+Juliet, *where Leonardo takes the magical love potion, that was influenced by the Mardi Gras.'* **Baz Luhrmann, film-maker**

It's easy to be a serial socialite in Sydney as the city's diary is choked with events every night of the week. Tourism New South Wales has the latest info on city events. Phone 13 20 77 and visit www.visitnsw.com.au.

The Sydney Festival—January

Web: www.sydneyfestival.org.au
An annual event which showcases both local and international talent—from performers to plays—in various venues around the city.

Australia Day—26 January

Web: www.australiaday.gov.au
Fireworks and tall ships help mark the day when the first white people arrived in Sydney in 1788. The Big Day Out music festival is staged in Homebush and features local and international acts.

Sony TropFest—February/March

Web: www.tropinc.com
This short and free film festival in the Domain attracts big name celebrity judges and entries from all over the country.

Sydney Gay & Lesbian Mardi Gras—Feb/March

Web: www.mardigras.org.au

Sydney's streets are blocked for a wild and wonderful night when the gay community fills the city with floats during a colourful parade.

Australian Fashion Week—May

Web: www.afw.com.au

Forget about attending this glamorous event unless you are well connected. Held each year at the Overseas Passenger Terminal, local designers hold parades, attended by international buyers and press.

City to Surf—August

Web: city2surf.sunherald.com.au

Thousands take to the streets for this 14-kilometre run in August each year, which is one of the largest timed foot races in the world.

Spring Racing Carnival—September to November

Web: www.ajc.com.au and www.stc.com.au

The annual social event of the national calendar, the Melbourne Spring Racing Carnival is a glamorous affair attracting magnates, fashionistas, international celebrities and the racing fraternity who descend on Flemington Race Course for the 'race that stops a nation'. In Sydney, offices host Melbourne Cup lunches, and five-star lunches are held at the city's top hotels and restaurants on the second Tuesday in November for this all afternoon affair.

Christmas—25 December

Web: www.cultureandrecreation.gov.au/articles/christmas

Aussie celebs flock home for Christmas with their families. Most have Christmas lunch at home (seafood, roast turkey and Christmas fruit pudding), but local hotels always put on a show. Palm Beach is the location of choice for the eastern suburbs set, with some rental homes commanding over $15,000 a week for a short stay.

Sydney to Hobart Yacht Race—26 December

Web: www.rolexsydneyhobart.com

One of Sydney Harbour's greatest annual spectacles, the racing fleet gather in Sydney Harbour on Boxing Day for the great race to Hobart.

New Year's Eve—31 December

Web: www.cityofsydney.nsw.gov.au/nye

A truly magnificent display in the Harbour, focussed around the Harbour Bridge, with fireworks at 9 pm and again at midnight.

Arts & Icons

'*The theatrical community in Australia, in Sydney, are a large part of who we are.*' **Cate Blanchett , actor**

Sydney has a strong artistic and thespian community so you just never know who you might see at an exhibition launch, theatre opening or one of the city's places of interest.

Sydney Opera House

Bennelong Point, Circular Quay

Phone: (02) 9250 7111 *Web:* www.sydneyoperahouse.com

Little did Danish architect Jorn Utzon know when he entered his submission into the New South Wales Government competition to design the Sydney Opera House that his winning entry would become one of the most recognisable and photographed landmarks of the modern world. Symbolic of Australia and showcasing a diverse spectrum of performing arts and high culture, its forecourt has staged concerts such as Crowded House's 'Farewell to the World' concert in 1996 (to which 120,000 people turned up). Coldplay performed in the Studio theatre for 150 fans and Chris Martin joked that the small intimate gig was like being demoted to the basement. The forecourt was also the focus of global attention during the 2000 Sydney Olympic Games when the the triathlon made its Olympic competition debut, and Australia's Michellie Jones took out the silver medal in the women's race. Notably, Arnold Schwarzennegger also won his final Mr Olympia Bodybuilding title in the Concert Hall in 1980.

In 2005, the Sydney Opera House was also the venue for the marriage of Australian soapie star Bec Cartwright and Aussie tennis ace Lleyton Hewitt. The reaction to Bec and Lleyton Hewitt's wedding was one of the greatest the Opera House has ever seen as the media battled to get wedding footage. One of the city's most renowned silver-service dining institutions, Guillaume at Bennelong, is also here: see index.

Celeb Scoop: *The Matrix Revolution's* premiere was held here in 2003. One of the most elaborate events to ever be staged in Sydney, the event is estimated to have cost over $1 million. During the film, Nicky and Paris Hilton fidgeted incessantly, kept disappearing to the restroom and then left after just 40 minutes, reappearing later at the afterparty. *The Crocodile Hunter: Collision Course* premiered here in 2002. Steve Irwin arrived with wife Terri and daughter Bindi, throwing both over his shoulder to walk the red carpet. This was after riding into the forecourt standing on the top of his truck and jumping off!

Sydney Harbour Bridge and BridgeClimb

5 Cumberland Street, The Rocks

Phone: (02) 8274 7777 *Web:* www.bridgeclimb.com.au
Sydneysiders might think little more of the Harbour Bridge other than that it serves an important purpose—linking the south side of the city to the north. But ever since it was opened in 1932, it has held the prized title of the world's largest steel arch bridge. Costing $20 million and taking nine years to build, 1400 workers were involved in its construction. Legendary actor Paul Hogan (of **Crocodile Dundee** fame) even worked as a rigger on the Bridge while waiting for his big break.

In 1998, BridgeClimb began operating climbing tours of the Harbour

Bridge. Tours run every 10 minutes from sunrise to sunset. Among those to have donned the grey climbing suit to partake in the three-and-a-half-hour climb are Justin Timberlake, Cameron Diaz, Crown Prince Frederik and Crown Princess Mary of Denmark, Pink, Prince Harry, Owen Wilson, Mandy Moore, Kate Bosworth, Keith Urban and Australia's own princess of pop, Kylie Minogue. You can see many famous faces in the photos on the wall at BridgeClimb HQ.

> Celeb Scoop: Former James Bond star Pierce Brosnan was banned from BridgeClimb in 2002. Having spent an afternoon having vodka martinis, a BridgeClimb breath test deemed him to be over the blood alcohol limit to safely complete the climb. All the 007 agent got was a cup of coffee and some fruit!

Sydney Theatre Company and the Wharf

Hickson Road, Walsh Bay

Phone: (02) 9250 1777 *Web:* www.sydneytheatre.com.au
A multi-million-dollar redevelopment has transformed the old Walsh Bay wharves into luxury apartments. Nicole Kidman bought one here in 2006, paying $4 million for her new digs. Matching this high-end 'tsjuzing', and adding to the area's celebrity kudos, is the Sydney Theatre, a $40-million performance space that Sydney's premier theatrical company, the Sydney Theatre Company, shares with the Australian Ballet and the Sydney Dance Company. Many talented performers have trod the boards of this 850-seat theatre including Cate Blanchett, who was recently appointed co-creative director of Sydney Theatre Company with her writer/director husband Andrew Upton. Across the road, the company's head office is housed in a historic 200-metre timber wharf, home to the indigenous dance group, Bangarra Dance Theatre, and the stunning Wharf restaurant.

Harry's Cafe de Wheels

Cowper Wharf, Cowper Wharf Road, Woolloomooloo
Web: www.harryscafedewheels.com.au

This tiny fast-food outlet has been serving up signature items like pies 'n' peas and hot dogs for almost as long as the Cowper Wharf pier has been in existence. A quintessential late-night Sydney experience for anyone about to head home after a night on the town, the lines here are always five people deep.

Harry's got its name in 1945, after the World War II soldier Harry 'Tiger' Edwards gave the eatery its first humble beginnings, selling pies from the back of his van. A detour here might find you squirting tomato sauce alongside any of the A-listers who still eat carbs every now and then—Rolf Harris, Kylie Minogue, Jason Biggs, Hilary Duff, Olivia Newton-John and Sir Elton John have all been photographed and their happy snaps are proudly displayed on the eatery's walls.

Art Gallery of New South Wales

Art Gallery Road, Sydney
Phone: (02) 9225 1744 *Web:* www.artgallery.nsw.gov.au

Opened in 1874, the Art Gallery of New South Wales houses some of the finest works of Australian artists like Margaret Preston, Sidney Nolan and Brett Whiteley. They also have an amazing collection of Aboriginal and Asian works. Each year the gallery is inundated with celebrity faces when the entries for the prestigious Archibald Prize portraiture competition begin to flood in.

> Celeb Scoop: Memorable portraits include those of actors Jack Thompson, David Wenham and Toni Collette, singer Paul Kelly and former Midnight Oil front man, Peter Garrett.

Museum of Sydney

Cnr Phillip and Bridge Sts, Sydney

Phone: (02) 9251 5988 *Web:* www.hht.net.au

Built on the foundations of the first Government House, this is the place to glean a snapshot of Sydney since 1788 through exhibitions, art, film and displays.

Powerhouse Museum

500 Harris Street, Ultimo

Phone: (02) 9217 0111 *Web:* www.powerhousemuseum.com

The largest museum in Australia, since 1988 this modern museum has the best of science, design and technology for all tastes and ages. It's hip, it's up-to-date, and the exhibitions are constantly changing. Forget musty displays of stuffed animals—this museum's got sex appeal!

Australian National Maritime Museum

2 Murray Street, Darling Harbour

Phone: (02) 9298 3777 *Web:* www.anmm.gov.au

Packed with Aussie maritime history, from historic ships to maritime treasures, this is a must-see for fans of the open sea—young and old.

Museum of Contemporary Art

140 Hickson Road, The Rocks

Phone: (02) 9245 2400 *Web:* www.mca.com.au

This stunning Art Deco building dates back to the 1950s and has one of the best waterfront positions of any art gallery. The works of

Australian artists have lined the walls of the MCA, along with pop art creations of Andy Warhol.

Celeb Scoop: It was during here press conference at the MCA in 2004 that Christina Aguilera revealed that it wasn't only Kylie Minogue who has a nice derriere in the music business: 'Good bums come in all shapes and sizes,' she said. Australian media weren't as impressed with Justin Timberlake's press conference—he was visiting with his then girlfriend Cameron Diaz and requested that no questions were to be asked about his personal life.

Restaurants

'I might be biased but I rate Australia as having some of the best food in the world... everything is fresher and the tastes are much stronger and purer.' **Naomi Watts, actor**

You're always guaranteed a table when you're famous and in the case of Sydney's celebrity chefs, it seems you're always certain of celebrity clientele.

Guillaume at Bennelong

Bennelong Point, Sydney

Phone: (02) 9241 1999 *Web:* www.guillaumeatbennelong.com.au
Along with its concert halls and performance spaces, the Opera House has one of the city's most renowned silver service dining institutions. Operated by one of the city's gold gilded chefs, Guillaume Brahimi, the Parisian native has created top end modern Australian food, a decadent wine list, in what is surely Sydney's most beautiful dinner venue.

Celeb Scoop: It was used as the official Robbie Williams afterparty venue for his 2006 tour. Guests were notified of the top secret location on the day of the event via SMS. Though the man himself did not attend, his best friend, UK star Max Beezly and many local identities, including media man James Packer's current wife Erica Baxter and former wife Jodhi Meares, did. Similiarly, when Aussie tennis star Lleyton Hewitt married *Home and Away* soapie starlet Bec Cartwright, their wedding guests weren't made aware of the ceremony venue until one hour before it began. Cricketer Shane Warne is a regular patron, usually ducking out regularly for a cigarette break during courses.

Icebergs Dining Room and Bar

1 Knotts Ave, Bondi

Phone: (02) 9365 9000 *Web:* www.idrb.com

Sitting at the southernmost point of Bondi Beach, Icebergs sits perched above an ocean-filled swimming pool with a bird's eye view of one of the world's most famous beaches. The hottest of Bondi's hot spots, what started out (and is still) a local swimming club now attracts the sexiest of Sydney's social set, especially during summer at sunset. Jack Nicholson, John Farnham, Portia de Rossi, Heath Ledger, Heather Graham, Owen Wilson and Tom Jones have all eaten here. Billy Crystal, *Little Britain* stars David Williams and Matt Lucas have all indulged in a latenight supper. Nicole Kidman regularly orders the oysters and fresh line-caught fish. Birthday parties for *Superman Returns* cast members, including director Bryan Singer were also held at Icebergs during the filming of the movie, along with weekly Sunday drinks sessions at sunset.

Celeb Scoop: Paris Hilton was reportedly paid up to $5 million by advertising magnate John Singleton for her whirlwind six-day promotional visit to Oz in 2006 with her only official media engagement—judging the Bondi Blonde (beer) competition—taking place at Bondi Icebergs. But her trip to Bondi almost never happened, however, as Paris began her Sydney visit with a blonde moment of her own—arriving two hours late because she forgot to take her passport to Los Angeles International Airport.

Nicole Kidman celebrated her 40th birthday in 2007 four days early with a pre-birthday gathering with 30 friends on June 16. Guests including sister Antonia and mother Janelle enjoyed a sit down dinner followed by birthday cake and candles. Though she mightn't look her age, Nicole did call on her friends to help blow all those candles out.

Aria

1 Macquarie Street, Sydney

Phone: (02) 9252 2555 *Web:* www.ariarestaurant.com

Boasting one of Sydney's best views—straight across the Opera House forecourt, the food here is as good as the vista. Celeb chef Matt Moran, makes each meal a designer-food experience and since it opened in late 1999, it has been a fave of many stars including Mel Gibson, Michael Caine, Jane Fonda, Priscilla Presley, Kim Cattrall, Will Smith, Keanu Reeves, Harry Connick Jnr, Chris Rock, KD Lang, Christina Aguilera, Michael Leunig, Mandy Moore, Ewan McGregor, Alice Cooper, Tim Rice, David Essex, Julian Lloyd-Webber, Baz Luhrmann, Jerry O'Connell, Mark Waugh and Steve Waugh.

Celeb Scoop: When Harrison Ford and Calista Flockhart dined here, Ford and his pint-sized fiancée soaked up the restaurant's famous views while dining on the seven course dinner tasting menu with matching wines. Flockhart enjoyed the indulgent selection of produce ranging from Sydney rock oysters to Bangalow sweet pork belly. The famous couple left before dessert was served, but not empty-handed, they took home a take-away cheese plate. Tom Cruise and Penelope Cruz made a dinner party affair of it in 2001, when they dined with director Cameron Crowe, James Packer and his then wife Jodhi, and Ray Martin and his daughter Jenna. Penelope ordered asparagus salad and then freshly shucked oysters, and Tom ate roasted John Dory. In 2001, John Travolta dined with Hugh Jackman and wife Deborra-Lee Furness on fillet mignon

Rossini with potato galette and bordelaise sauce. Monica Bellucci and Vincent Cassell have dined here three times, and on one occasion, Laurence Fishbourne was also dining on the same night—hence a lot of movie chat between tables. Monica ordered rolled roasted Kangaroo Island chicken with a nori and chicken stuffing, miso and truffle broth.

Cowper Wharf Restaurant Strip

Cowper Wharf, Cowper Wharf Road, Woolloomooloo

• **Otto** Phone: (02) 9368 7488

Web: www.ottoristorante.com.au

• **Salon Blanc** Phone: (02) 9356 2222

Web: www.salonblanc.com.au

• **China Doll** Phone: (02) 9380 6744

Web: www.chinadoll.com.au

• **Kingsley's Steak and Crabhouse** Phone: 1300 546 475

Web: www.kingsleys.com.au

• **Nove Cucina** Phone: (02) 9368 7599

Web: www.otto.net.au

• **Manta** Phone: (02) 9332 3822

Web: www.mantaresaturant.com.au

For celebrity-spotting, lunchtime is ideal to visit any of the acclaimed restaurants that line the city facing strip of the Woolloomooloo wharf. Media magnate John Laws used to own part of Otto, but his share has since been sold to Leon Fink (restaurateur of Quay fame). Otto is a favourite of Australia's number one female radio personality, Jackie O, who dined here with her parents and partner Lee Henderson on the eve of their wedding in 2003. Other stars who have frequented the wharfside restaurants include Jessica Simpson, Sandra Bullock, Jennifer Hawkins, Megan Gale, Owen Wilson and Paul Walker.

Celeb Scoop: Whenever Naomi Watts is in town, she dines at Otto. Kingsley's is a favourite of singer/songwriter Alex Lloyd, and also of cricketer Greg Matthews. Russell Crowe dines at China Doll. In December 2004, Russ shared two bottles of wine with friends totalling almost $2000! In 2007, when Salon Blanc first opened, Kylie Minogue was one of the first to dine here, along with funny man Sasha Baron Cohen, Westlife and Sarah Murdoch.

Tetsuya's

529 Kent Street, Sydney

Phone: (02) 9267 2900 ***Web:*** www.tetsuyas.com

Regularly named as one of the best restaurants in the world, this restaurant in a low-key setting in the city is all about the food. Celebrities dine here for an intimate experience away from prying eyes of the paparazzi. The degustation menu or tasting menu is the order of the day, and the masterful techniques chef Tetsuya Wakuda uses to combine the best of Japanese, French and anything else he is inspired by makes this a dining experience to savour, and remember.

Celeb Scoop: When Natalie Imbruglia craves modern Asian cuisine while she's in Sydney, this is one of her favourite places to go.

Est

252 George Street Sydney

Phone: (02) 9240 3010 ***Web:*** www.merivale.com

Located in the trendy Establishment complex, this flagship restaurant continues to amaze. Striking Corinthian columns, chandeliers, and elegant cream and almond colours complement a menu which includes simple yet appealing food. Elle McPherson, Mischa Barton, Heath Ledger and Jay Kay have all been left satisfied here.

Celeb Scoop: Nicole Kidman and her sister Antonia like to have lunch here when Nic jets back into town. English socialite India Hicks flew in from the Carribean to host a lunch here in 2007, to launch her range of Crabtree & Evelyn beauty products.

Catalina Rose Bay

1 Sunderland Avenue, Lyne Park, Rose Bay

Phone: (02) 9371 0555 *Web:* www.catalinarosebay.com.au
Described as 'Sydney's verandah', this is one of Sydney's best fine
dining restaurants. Sublime views stretch right over the water and
the famous Sydney to Hobart yacht race starts directly in front of the
restaurant. Frequented regularly by celebrities, including a resident
penguin who has become an identity in his own right.

Celeb Scoop: Lachlan Murdoch hosted a dinner here for Will
Smith during his visit to attend the premiere of *I, Robot* in 2004.
Cindy Crawford sampled the seafood here at lunchtime during
her 2007 promo visit to open Omega's flagship store.

The Pier

594 New South Head Road, Rose Bay

Phone: (02) 9327 6561 *Web:* www.pierrestaurant.com.au
Pier is one of only a handful of Sydney restaurants awarded the Oscar
of Australia's culinary world—three chefs hats by the *Sydney Morning
Herald's Good Food Guide.* Only the freshest seafood is chosen to
create the most sublime meals.

Celeb Scoop: Jerry Hall enjoyed a long lunch here ordering
big on the seafood during her stint in Sydney to strut her stuff
on the catwalk during Australian Fashion Week in 2000 (see
index). Princess Mary lunched here during a visit to Sydney in
2005, with her good friend Amber Petty.

*'Pier was my favourite restaurant in Sydney. It's right on Rose
Bay and the restaurant just juts out into the harbour, it's shaped
like an old, beautiful boat. In fact, you can dock outside of the
restaurant and then come up for lunch.'* **Kate Bosworth, actor**

Longrain

85 Commonwealth Street, Surry Hills

Phone: (02) 9280 2888 *Web:* www.longrain.com

A unique Thai dining experience if you've never eaten at a shared table (with strangers). Funnily enough, celebrities do eat here—but many favour the private dining room on the right hand side of the restaurant which seats around 12.

Rockpool

107 George Street, The Rocks

Phone: (02) 9252 1888 *Web:* www.rockpoolsydney.com

Neil Perry has certainly cooked for all of the stars as his various restaurants have come and gone over the years, however this one, his original, has been serving upmarket, stylised food for more than 15 years. It's more like a theatrical experience. Even the menu will educate you about Australian cuisine and how it is harvested, prepared and so on.

Celeb Scoop: Stars who have dined here include Aussie chef Curtis Stone who enjoys a meal here when he returns to Sydney.

Bistro Moncur

116 Queen Street, Woollahra

Phone: (02) 9363 2519 *Web:* www.woollahrahotel.com.au

A favourite with visiting celebrities as well as Sydney's regular A-list, Damien Pignolet's Bistro Moncur is a Sydney institution. The place has a touch of France about it, but sitting in the heart of Sydney's A-list belt, the menu, food and wine list is quintessential Australia. Portions are large, and dishes are full-flavoured, and some of Sydney's best seafood, meat and desserts are on offer.

Celeb Scoop: Former Prime Minister Paul Keating has been seen lunching here, along with a plethora of local TV faces.

Claude's

10 Oxford Street, Paddington

Phone: (02) 9331 2325 *Web:* www.claudes.com.au

Sitting among Oxford Street's boutiques, this is a far cry from the modernity of many of Sydney's dining spots, Claude's only seats 40, but the well known and locals flock here for fine, modern French food. Gorgeous for dinner, as you'll really feel like a VIP here.

Ocean Room

Overseas Passenger Terminal, Circular Quay West, The Rocks

Phone: (02) 8273 1277 *Web:* www.oceanroomsydney.com

Ocean Room is aptly named because of its prime waterside location and, as you would expect, the restaurant includes some top level seafood selections on its menu. There is a private dining room on its second level, which has been used for many A-list parties and events. Bette Midler, Carey Otis and Prince Harry are a few of the celeb patrons.

Celeb Scoop: Prince Harry jumped behind the bar and started serving drinks during a party for the World Cup Rugby a few years back. Sony/BMG used Ocean Room as the venue of a special lunch with 'popera' super group Il Divo, who arrived at the restaurant via speedboat. UK band Blue have also enjoyed a shooter or two at the private bar.

Wildfire

Overseas Passenger Terminal, Circular Quay West, The Rocks

Phone: (02) 8273 1222 *Web:* www.wildfiresydney.com

Wildfire is one of Sydney's most exclusive restaurants. The towering dining room filled with huge glamorous chandeliers belies the intimate service and diverse menu. The food is nothing short of five-star, and dining here would typically mean you're dining alongside some of the world's most famous people. Diners here have included Elle Macpherson, Richard Branson, Sylvester Stallone, Tom Jones, Erica

Bana, Linda Evangalista and Hilary Duff.

Celeb Scoop: When Cameron Diaz, Drew Barrymore and Lucy Liu were staying at the Park Hyatt to promote *Charlie's Angels 2: Full Throttle*, they dined at Wildfire and loved the globe artichoke soup so much they ordered it in as room service to their hotel rooms at the Park Hyatt the next night.

Doyles at the Quay

Overseas Passenger Terminal, George Street, The Rocks
Phone: (02) 9252 3400 *Web:* www.doyles.com.au
Doyles has a solid reputation for having some of the best fish and chips in Sydney. Right at the far end of the Overseas Passenger Terminal, it boasts views of both of Sydney's iconic attractions: the Sydney Harbour Bridge and the Sydney Opera House.

Quay

Overseas Passenger Terminal, George Street, The Rocks
Phone: (02) 9251 5600 *Web:* www.quay.com.au
Another flawless Sydney location overlooking the harbour, food here is top shelf in every respect, with service and a wine list to match. Chef Peter Gilmore's speciality is a stunning degustation with matching wines, one of Australia's finest culinary experiences.

Celeb Scoop: Actor Sandra Bullock dined here when she was in town to promote *Miss Congeniality 2: Armed and Fabulous*. Australian PMs, Billy Joel, Elton John, Billy Connolly, Elle MacPherson and U2 have all eaten here.

Glass Brasserie

Sydney Hilton, 488 George Street, Sydney
Phone: (02) 9266 2000 *Web:* www.hiltonsydney.com.au
Don't be put off by the fact this restaurant is in a hotel. Chef Luke Mangan was flown to Denmark to create the wedding menu of Crown

Prince Frederik and Princess Mary. He was also flown to prepare meals for Richard Branson on one of his own islands and also chosen by Nicole Kidman to cater for her wedding guests in 2006. He has been the face, name and chef behind this restaurant since the Hilton Sydney opened its doors following a complete revamp in 2006. The towering glass interiors reportedly cost $6 million, and are truly striking, with huge glass windows, towering ceilings, and a modern decadence including a separate lift to bring patrons in from George Street.

Celeb Scoop: Jessica and Ashlee Simpson weren't impressed with the fine dining menu—that includes wagyu steak and quails eggs—on offer at Glass during their trip to Sydney for the MTV VMAs in 2006. Instead of ordering from the menu, they chose to order in a pizza—a large pepperoni and double cheese. Soccer star Harry Kewell has also dined here with the head man himself, Luke Mangan.

Machiavelli Ristorante Italian

123 Clarence Street, Sydney

Phone: (02) 9299 3748 *Web:* www.machiavelli.com.au
This is the ultimate place for the Sydney 'power lunch'. Famous faces all flock to this basement Italian joint to be served simple food by aging but charming waiters. Check out the wall hangings filled with famous Aussie faces.

Celeb Scoop: Its unassuming location appeals to Kylie Minogue who has often popped in for lunch, sometimes with her mother. Barry Humphries, Rupert Murdoch and James Packer are other famous faces who have also been seen here.

Cafe Sydney

Level 5, Customs House, 31 Alfred Street, The Rocks

Phone: (02) 9252 8683 *Web:* www.cafesydney.com
This is the place where celebs come to soak up not only the fantastic cuisine, but also the breathtaking views of Sydney Harbour from the

quayside balcony. The historic sandstone Customs House building in which Cafe Sydney is located dates back to the late 1800s.

Celeb Scoop: Jennifer Aniston and Vince Vaughn shared an intimate seafood meal here after 'avoiding' each other on the red carpet for the premiere of *The Break Up*. During the meal, Vaughn left Aniston at the table three times to have a cigarette.

The Summit Restaurant and Orbit Lounge

Level 47, Australia Square, 264 George Street, Sydney

Phone: (02) 9247 9777 *Web:* www.summitrestaurant.com.a

Sitting right at the top of the Harry Seidler-designed Australia Square—which is actually round in shape, not square—this is the place to see Sydney in all its glory as this restaurant offers 360-degree views of the city. Best of all, you don't have to move to take in the sights—sit back in your seat while the restaurant actually revolves gently (a complete revolution takes two hours).

Celeb Scoop: Following the Australian premiere of *Men In Black II*, a lavish afterparty was held in the Summit Restaurant. Lara Flynn Boyle requested the restaurant stop revolving, as it made her feel sick. Management obliged her request—for the first and only time in the restaurant's history.

Forty One Restaurant

2 Chifley Square, Sydney

Phone: (02) 9221 2500 *Web:* www.forty-one.com.au

In the heart of corporate Sydney at the top of Chifley Tower, Forty One is one of Sydney's classic places to dine. The menu features varied gourmet Australian dishes, created by chef and owner Dietmar Sawyere. For a real taste of celebrity treatment, book one of the restaurant's two private dining rooms.

Altitude

Level 36, 176 Cumberland Street, The Rocks

Phone: (02) 9221 2500 *Web:* www.altitudesydney.com.au

First class views mix with the best in cocktails and cuisine at Shangri-La's top level fine diner. And how's this for the ultimate VIP dining experience: a private dining room with a glass floor!

Celeb Scoop: During Fashion Week one year, the floor in the private dining room bore the brunt of too many stilettos, and was left quite dented the next morning.

Hotels

'I stayed at The Quay Grand Suites Sydney—right on the harbour. My view overlooked the Opera House and the Sydney Harbour Bridge.' **Kate Bosworth, actor**

The number one rule for celebrities when checking into a hotel: always use an unassuming alias. Jack Black used Stanley Kubrick (the name of the famous film director) when here to promote *School of Rock* and Matt Damon used Jason Bourne (the name of his *Bourne Supremacy* character).

The Park Hyatt

7 Hickson Road, Sydney

Phone: (02) 9241 1234 *Web:* www.sydney.park.hyatt.com

If the walls of Park Hyatt could talk, they really would have some interesting tales to tell. The who's who of Hollywood have all stayed here on their various visits to Sydney and experienced what it's like to wake up to a full frontal view of the Harbour Bridge and Opera House. The presidential suite comes with separate quarters for bodyguards. For many years, the hotel has been at the top of the preferred hotel list for the country's leading film and music companies. The Rolling Stones,

Bono, Robbie Williams, Elton John, Greg Norman, Susan Sarandon, Owen Wilson, Kate Hudson, Vin Diesel, Heather Graham, Morgan Freeman, Renee Zellweger, Charlize Theron, Stuart Townsend, Heath Ledger, Michelle Williams, and Naomi Watts have all stayed here.

Celeb Scoop: Tom Cruise once stayed here with wife Katie and remained committed to his Scientology faith, refraining from alcohol and eating small meals. Hotel staff had to black out the windows of the presidential suite for John Travolta in 2004 'to avoid prying eyes' and when Cher stayed here, she requested so many packets of M&Ms, she couldn't eat them all. Patrick Swayze got hotel staff to take him to see some live Australian music. Wearing a baseball hat and glasses, Swayze was taken incognito to see Midnight Oil at the Enmore Theatre (see index). Sandra Bullock loves the choc chip cookies on the room service menu, even serving them up to journalists during her media engagements for *Miss Congeniality 2* in 2004. Nicollette Sheridan's Hestia launch luncheon was held here in 2005. One of the more controversial guests was Sylvester Stallone in 2007. After being held up at Sydney Airport in customs after 48 vials of banned growth hormones were located in his luggage, he and his entourage were later reported to have thrown more vials of the illegal substance out of their hotel windows prior to an official room search. Sly told customs officers that 'doing Rambo is hard work' and was later fined $2,975 for bringing banned substances into the country.

The Establishment Hotel

5 Bridge Lane, Sydney

Phone: (02) 9240 3000 *Web:* www.merivale.com/establishment
If harbour views aren't a priority, this is about as slick as Sydney gets. Accessed through a discreet entrance on Bridge Lane, the 35 hotel rooms are modern with a choice of light or dark colour scheme.

Celeb Scoop: Usher, Robbie Williams, Jay Kay, Tina Arena, Scissor Sisters, Laurence Fishburne, Heather Graham, Jeremy Irons, Mandy Moore and Dannii Minogue have all been guests here. If you want to feel like the biggest of stars, check into one of the Establishment's two penthouses as Barry White and Sting did. Kate Bosworth stayed in the duplex penthouse during her time in Sydney filming *Superman Returns*. Checked in under the name 'Miss Torstar' Kate's penthouse apartment was spread over two levels, featuring a massive king-sized bed on the lower level and open plan living and dining areas on the upper.

Hotel InterContinental

Corner Bridge and Phillip Sts, Sydney

Phone: (02) 9253 9000 *Web:* www.ichotelsgroup.com

The InterContinental's super swish Australia Suite has hosted stars including Frank Sinatra, Liza Minelli, Sammy Davis Junior, former President Bill Clinton, Al Gore, Prince, Pavarotti, Paloma Picasso, Jerry Hall, Jennifer Aniston, Vince Vaughn, Pierce Brosnan, Sylvester Stallone, Diana Ross, Britney Spears and Matt Damon.

Celeb Scoop: Frank Sinatra and his wife at the time, Barbara, stayed here in 1989, checking in accompanied by a police escort. Barbara brought 30 different hair pieces with her and spread them over a table in the room while Frank requested a local deli to open at 2am to fulfil his craving for salami. Pavarotti liked to cook his own pasta each night, and had new pots and pans and kitchen accessories brought in. Mel Gibson smoked cigarettes on the balcony with hotel staff in 2000. Prince insisted on purple drapes, and slept in purple sheets. John Travolta worked out in the hotel gym every day with his own trainer from the US. Matt Damon was asked by his film publicity company to pen a personalised note to Delta Goodrem on a *Bourne Supremacy* poster in 2004. Nicole Kidman and Keith

Urban spent around $200,000 dollars at the hotel that included 40 rooms to accommodate guests attending their wedding in 2005 and a $200 credit for guests to use their minibar and other services. When US President Bill Clinton stayed, he and his staff took over two floors, bringing in their own photocopiers, paper shredders and telephones. A service lift had to be fitted out with wood panelling and carpet so he could enter his suite directly from the underground car park. Bulletproof panels were fitted to the front of the windows. Barbra Streisand *didn't* stay here after being told her request for new white carpets to be laid in the Australia Suite was not possible. Chris Isaak gatecrashed a wedding here and ended up serenading the newlywed couple with his song *Wicked Game*. During her single days, Nicole Kidman was reportedly serenaded by an international pursuer on the top floor, who presented her with a diamond bracelet. In 2005, Vince Vaughn and Jennifer Aniston fronted a packed room of media to promote *The Break-Up*. At the time, Vaughn and Aniston were rumoured to be dating but in a bid to dispel any such allegations, the pair appeared at separate times. Aniston's famous poker-straight hair was courtesy of a blowdry from her personal hairdresser, who she brought with her from the US. Aniston also spent considerable time in the hotel's gym.

Quay Grand

61 Macquarie Street, Sydney

Phone: (02) 9256 4000 *Web:* www.mirvachotels.com/quay-grand

The ultimate harbour-front address, Quay Grand is newer than many of the other hotel offerings. Michael Caine, Keanu Reeves, Paris Hilton, Hilary Duff and Australian actors Sarah Wynter and David Wenham are among some of the A-listers to have checked in here.

Celeb Scoop: It was here in 2004 that Hilary Duff revealed that if she was granted any one wish, it would be for 400 pairs of Marc Jacobs shoes. Other celeb requests have included bowls of M&Ms in certain colours only, pegs to hang up wigs and blacked out windows to soothe paranoia fears of the paparazzi climbing the walls to take photos! Ronn Moss and fellow *Bold and the Beautiful* actors Katherine Kelly Lang, Mackenzie Mauzy and Kyle Lowder stayed here during the filming of the show's special twentieth anniversary episodes which were shot in and around Sydney.

Shangri-La

176 Cumberland Street, Sydney

Phone: (02) 9250 6000 ***Web:*** www.shangri-la.com

Renovated in 2005, this five-star, high rise hotel is as glamorous it gets, complete with flawless harbour views from level 36 from the Horizon Bar and Aria Restaurant (see index). Sean Connery, royalty, and politicians stay here. Previously known as the ANA, the 563 guestrooms have quality furniture, sheets and fittings, as well as all of the luxuries you'd expect from a top city hotel.

Celeb Scoop: Prince Frederik and Princess Mary stayed here during their visit in March 2005. Omega checked in their ambassador Cindy Crawford here for her 2007 visit. During her stay, Cindy requested Evian water, mint tea, bananas and fresh roses in her room.

'*The Shangri-La Hotel Sydney is right across from the Opera House and the Harbour Bridge. I've never stayed there, but the views are supposed to be great.*' **Natalie Imbruglia, singer/songwriter**

Sofitel Wentworth Hotel

61-101 Phillip Street, Sydney

Phone: (02) 9230 0700 ***Web:*** www.sofitel.com

This hotel has quite a celebrity history, even including hosting the

Queen. It was Sydney's first ever five star hotel, and has had several name changes and make-overs. The latest was a $60 million make-over in 2005.

Celeb Scoop: The most famous moment under the hotel's roof, was probably when Prince Charles and Princess Diana danced in the ballroom during an Australian visit in 1983.

Four Seasons Sydney

199 George Street, Sydney

Phone: (02) 9238 0000 *Web:* www.fourseasons.com

Believe it or not, this hotel is built on the site where the First Fleet's convicts set up camp in 1788. Fomerly known as The Regent, today it accommodates some of Sydney's highest profile visitors from all over the world. Jerry Hall, Michael Jackson, Tom Cruise, Neil Diamond, Kevin Costner, The Osbournes, Anna Nicole Smith and Carmen Electra have experienced first-hand the slick Italian marble bathrooms, and delux furniture that fill the 531 rooms and suites.

Celeb Scoop: Tom Cruise and Nicole Kidman went jogging in Hyde Park from their base of The Regent hotel every morning around 6am and one day asked the hotel to send out for real draught Guinness on tap from Kitty O'Shea's. The stars, who obviously acquired a taste for Guinness while filming *Far and Away* in Ireland, received four schooners with Glad Wrap covering the heads. Luciano Pavarotti stayed in the Regent Suite, and the chef arranged for pasta cooking equipment and the best pasta and sauce ingredients especially for Pavarotti so he could prepare his own meals, and he insisted his lemons should be quartered and not halved in his mineral water. Michael Jackson also stayed in the same suite when he was in Australia and asked for the suite's second bedroom to be turned into a dance floor so he could practise his dance moves. Michael had a video camera set up so he could film himself and threw cola on the dance floor to make it sticky. Neil Diamond and his crew insisted on having a table tennis room set up when they stayed and after performing they would return to the hotel room and play.

The Observatory Hotel

89-113 Kent Street, The Rocks

Phone: (02) 9256 2222 *Web:* www.observatoryhotel.com.au

The Observatory Hotel is a favourite with English famous faces and international royalty, as well as stars who want to keep their visit low key. You can imagine Ralph Fiennes sitting in the front bar enjoying tea, as it oozes classic English charm. Located in The Rocks a short stroll from Circular Quay, this hotel run by The Orient Express Group can make you feel as if you are stepping back in time with all of the modern accessories you would expect from a five star abode. There are 96 rooms including eight junior suites and 12 executive suites. The day spa and health club is one of the best in Sydney and stars love the La Prairie massages which leave their skin glowing. The Galileo restaurant is a hit, and the Globe Bar is sublime.

The Hilton Sydney

488 George Street, Sydney

Phone: (02) 9266 2000 *Web:* www.hiltonsydney.com.au

Even before we had heard of Paris and Nicky, the Hilton brand was always renowned for luxury and glamour. The Sydney hotel underwent an extensive refurbishment from 2002, and is today a place where Paris would surely break her rule of never staying in one of her family hotels. Special relaxation rooms come with a bath butler!

Celeb Scoop: Mischa Barton, Fergie, Good Charlotte, Sophie Monk and Miss Universe Jennifer Hawkins have stayed here post-refurbishment, as has Nicole Richie, who actually ate a lot of fresh fruit during her stay. In its earlier days, George Benson stayed here an had a special reason for getting out and about. He's a Jehovah's witness and spent his spare time door-knocking.

Sheraton On The Park

161 Elizabeth Street, Sydney

Phone: (O2) 9286 6000 *Web:* www.sheraton.com/sydney

Located directly opposite the city's Hyde Park, this hotel sits right among the city's shopping mecca. With 557 rooms, including 48 suites, there's always something happening here. Guests here have included Janet Jackson, Harry Connick Jnr, Michael Jackson, Ja Rule, Jamie Oliver, Barry Humphries, Jose Carreras, Natalia Imbruglia, Daniel Johns, Derek Lucas and Peter Berg.

Celeb Scoop: Paris Hilton checked in here for New Year's Eve in 2006 when she couldn't land a harbour view suite at any of the other hotels in town. This was also the venue for The Beatles' first ever Australian press conference in 1964.

Regents Court Hotel

18 Springfield Ave, Potts Point, Sydney

Phone: (O2) 9358 1533 *Web:* www.regentscourt.com.au

Run by the MacMahon family since 1990, this has been a celebrity spot for years. Writers, film directors and actors stay here. Located in the middle of Kings Cross, it is not for the faint hearted, as some of Sydney's most undesirables call the area home, but there is a unique charm about the place that keeps people—including well known ones coming back for more.

Medusa

267 Darlinghurst Road, Darlinghurst

Phone: (O2) 9331 1000 *Web:* www.medusa.com.au

The Medusa is one of Kylie's favourites, and is frequented by many other stars, particularly those who are in town for a long stay. Opened by well-known Sydney hotelliers Terry and Robert Schwamberg in 1998, this haven of modern opulent style is just gorgeous.

The Chelsea

10-14 Railway Street, Chatswood, Sydney

Phone: (02) 9411 4995

Located in one of the shopping jewels of Sydney, The Chelsea is a neat, French provincial style delight, with just 13 rooms. Authors and celebrities as well as fashion designers at the quirkier end of the scale like staying here, as the terrace-style buildings ooze charm and style, and guests quickly feel at home. The doubles have their own ensuites with showers and some even have original fireplaces. If shopping, and spotting fashionistas is in your agenda, you will love this well priced hotel.

Sir Stamford Double Bay
(formerly known as The Ritz Carlton)

22 Knox Street, Double Bay, Sydney

Phone: (02) 9302 4100 *Web:* www.stamford.com.au

At the time of going to print, this 140-room hotel had been sold for around $80 million and plans were underway to transform it into a luxury apartment block. In its golden years as the Ritz, it was one of the most decadent places for A-listers to rest their head and everyone from former US President Bill Clinton and John Travolta to Princess Diana and pop princess Kylie Minogue stayed here. Just after its opening, during 1991-1992, George Bush Snr booked out the entire hotel for three months over New Year's Eve. In 1993, Madonna had her room transformed into a gym. Former Australian PM Bob Hawke lived in room 531 for almost two years while he was in between marriages (word is he received mates rates from his owner friend).

Celeb Scoop: This is the hotel where INXS front man Michael Hutchence was found dead in his room, Suite 524, in 1997. The coroner ruled his death as suicide. His funeral was held at St Andrew's Cathedral (see index).

Blue Sydney

Cowper Wharf, 6 Cowper Wharf Road, Woolloomooloo

Phone: (02) 9331 9000 *Web:* www.tajhotels.com

If you've ever wanted to get into bed with the likes of Gisele Bunchen, Natalie Imbruglia, Paul Walker, Owen Wilson, Isla Fisher, Jason Biggs, Jesse Bradford, Robbie Williams or John Mayer, then the Blue Hotel is the place for you. The king-sized beds of this boutique hotel are renowned as being *the* best beds. A huge list of the world's biggest celebs rest their weary heads on Blue's European-sized goosedown pillows, slipping their overly flash-bulbed bodies between their 400 thread-count Egyptian cotton sheets. Room rates are high, but the uber-cool sophisticated look and feel of this hotel—not to mention the sensational water views—make it worth the expense.

Celeb Scoop: Nicollette Sheridan's room in the hotel was filled with roses for her birthday by her boyfriend Michael Bolton when she was in town for the announcement of her appointment as the face of Hestia. Also holed up in Blue for a naughty weekend in 2006 was Josh Hartnett and his *30 Days of Night* co-star Amber Sainsbury—controversial, because he was still with his Hollywood girlfriend, Scarlett Johansson, at the time.

The Sebel Pier One

Pier One, Hickson Road, The Rocks

Phone: (02) 8298 9999 *Web*: www.sebelpierone.com.au

Offering a little more privacy—and the chance of staying completely anonymously—The Sebel Pier One has the same spectacular views as the Park Hyatt a little bit further from the main hub of The Rocks' waterfront dining precinct. Uniquely, the 160-room hotel has its own pier-side pontoon and a 12-metre glass floor in the lobby.

Celeb Scoop: Actor Radha Mitchell loves the steamed green beans and French fries available in the restaurant here. She ate them in the restaurant and also ordered them to her room during her visit to Sydney to promote the film *Visitors*. Sophie Dahl and Jodie Kidd both stayed here on their respective trips to model at Mercedes Australian Fashion Week.

'You miss the familiarity of Australia—even when you've been in LA for years.... I miss the trees and the people and the pace because the people here move at a really nice pace.'
Radha Mitchell, actor

Sydney Harbour Marriott

30 Pitt Street, Sydney

Phone: (02) 9259 7000 *Web*: www.marriott.com.au

Formerly the Renaissance Hotel, the Sydney Harbour Marriott offers harbour views on one side and expansive city views on the other. Its central location makes it hard to beat.

Celeb Scoop: Bette Midler held her press conference here in 2005 and was quick to rule out teaming up with Britney Spears when one journalist asked her if the rumours regarding a movie collaboration with the US singer were true.

Swiss-Grand Resort and Spa

Cnr Campbell Pde and Beach Road, Bondi

Phone: (02) 9365 5666 *Web:* www.swissgrand.com.au

Situated right across from Bondi's famous beach and within easy walking distance to the plethora of dining and drinking venues in Bondi, the Swiss-Grand has hosted an array of famous faces.

Celeb Scoop: During the 2000 Olympic Games, the Brazilian beach volleyball teams—men's and women's—graced the Swiss Grand with their party-loving presence (and their finely honed physiques!).

Devere Hotel

44-46 Macleay Street, Potts Point

Phone: (02) 9358 1211 *Web:* www.devere.com.au

If you're after colourful stories about Kings Cross, the 24-hour concierge could probably tell you enough to write a book! They won't though, as they keep their guest list hush-hush. This is an intimate but basic 100-room boutique style hotel.

Kathryns on Queen

20 Queen Street, Woollahra

Phone: (02) 9327 4535 *Web:* www.kathryns.com.au

This National Trust listed Victorian terrace house was built around 1888 and operates as an exclusive B&B with only three rooms, making it a popular choice for stars and visiting politicians wishing to go incognito. Each room is decorated by the host, Kathryn Bruderiln, exquisitely appointed with fine linens, high comfy beds and fresh flowers. Try the Attic Suite for harbour glimpses and total privacy. Don't miss the healthy breakfasts with stewed fruit, eggs and fresh bread served either on your balcony, in the dining room or in the leafy courtyard.

Medina Executive Sydney Central

2 Lee Street, Haymarket

Phone: (02) 8396 9800 *Web*: www.medina.com.au

This heritage-listed hotel has been superbly restored and provides unparalleled access to all Sydney has to offer. Close ties to Sony/BMG Australia means there's often a muso checking in here.

Celeb Scoop: Not sure how his fiancée Katherine Heigl would feel, Josh Kelley had a dream about going to church with Sharon Stone when he stayed here in 2004. In the middle of his dream, Josh was awoken at 4.30am for a fire drill. Concerned with saving his laptop, he had no time to dress and evacuated wearing only his jocks and a jacket!

ON THE A-LIST

Sydney's Celebrity Hot Spots

Circular Quay & The Rocks

'I love Australia and Sydney in particular so much. I would love to go back. I miss it. I miss the water, the people and the food, and the cobblestones in an area called The Rocks.' Brittany Murphy, actor

This is where it all happens in Sydney. World-class views are the key attraction for celebrities to flock to **Circular Quay**, the heart of this famed Australian city, and those world-renowned iconic landmarks—the Sydney Opera House and Sydney Harbour Bridge—are a central part of this area's 'wow factor'.

Select upmarket and ultra-glam restaurants fill the inner harbour and few celebrities arrive in Sydney without spending some—if not most—of their time here. The heritage of a bygone era offered by **The Rocks** in particular also makes this one of the most historically and culturally rich regions of the city.

Among the famous faces listing at least one of their residential addresses as Circular Quay is controversial Australian radio commentator Alan Jones. Jones is a friend of the local rich and famous, and lives in Macquarie Street, inside the famous Bennelong apartment building. Fondly referred to as 'The Toaster' by many Sydneysiders, this is where Nicole Kidman stayed during a renovation to her Darling Point home. Fancy having her as a neighbour? A standard three-bedroom apartment can cost up to $6.5 million!

Kidman's latest property purchase is a penthouse at Sydney Harbour's **Walsh Bay** development. Kidman paid $4 million for a two-storey, three-bedroom security apartment soon after she married Keith Urban. Reportedly, her decision to purchase had much to do with the unfaltering paparazzi attention she experienced in the lead-up to her wedding in 2005. Photographers camped out on the doorstep

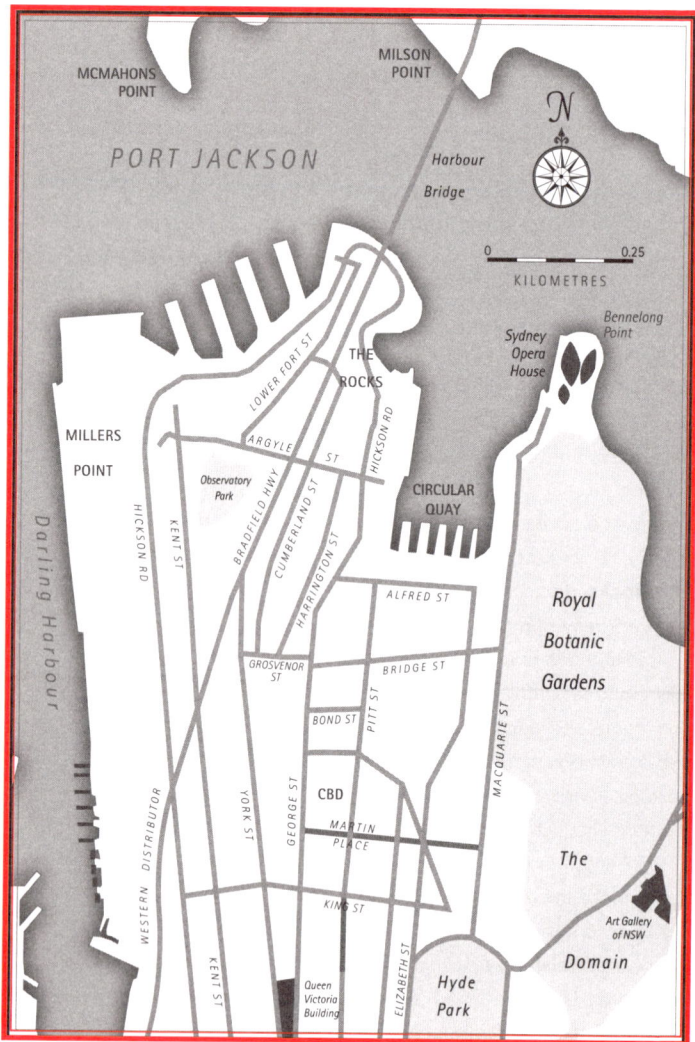

Circular Quay and The Rocks

of her Darling Point duplex, giving her no room to move at all, but it's much harder for even creative paparazzi to gain photography access to celebrities at her new residence, with a 24/7 concierge on duty, underground security carparks and no neighbouring backyards thanks to its finger wharf location.

Visiting celebrities, too, always seem to end up using The Rocks and Circular Quay as their home-away-from-home. The late Michael Hutchence often stayed at Quay West Apartments, and other big names including Frank Sinatra, Greg Norman, Billy Connelly, Tom Cruise, John Travolta, Bono, Cameron Diaz, Bill Clinton, Prince, Billy Joel and Prince have all stayed in hotels in the area following their concert performances, red-carpet film premieres or media interviews. Indeed, if you were lucky enough to be privy to the guest room lists, it is likely you would find some big names listed on the accommodation registers on any given night—though the majority of celebrities use aliases, of course.

The volume of big-name stars who regularly inhabit the hotels of the area also mean that you'll have a pretty good chance of bumping into some famous folk if you happen to be at one of the many restaurants, cafes, bars or shops located there. And with the ferry and Jet Cat wharves close by, you can be on the lookout even when you're on the water. So keep your eyes peeled—you could easily find yourself cruising the harbour towards Manly, ordering a drink at a bar with Robbie Williams, climbing the Harbour Bridge with Kylie Minogue or walking beside the harbour alongside Matt Damon or Renee Zellweger.

Shopping in The Rocks will also prove a treat as many celebrities fall in love with the cobblestone laneways and the haven of specialty stores, galleries and boutiques in the area. Aside from the Rocks Markets (which run every weekend), other hot shopping spots include Metcalfe Arcade, Nurses Walk, Playfair Street, Clocktower Square and George Street stores, as well as Gucci, Burberry, Ralph Lauren and many other international brand outlets. Argyle Place in The Rocks underwent an extreme makeover in 2007, with the multimillion dollar nightspot, The Argyle, opening its doors. Prior to that, it was also transformed into a quarter of Seville for *Mission Impossible: II* in the scenes where religious processions walked the streets to the sound of Spanish music.

A natural drawcard to the area is the **Royal Botanic Gardens**, one of the most beautiful places in Sydney for a walk. It's often used by high-profile names to keep fit, including Russell Crowe, who lives around the corner in Woolloomooloo (see index).

Hotels

'I had a really good time last time I was here in Sydney and I wanted to come back. At the time I was 31 years old and I had gone 31 years without ever checking this place out and I just remember thinking, 'I want to get my brother down here'. We took a little tour of the harbour yesterday and it was great. There is a lot of enthusiasm from the Damon camp for this place.' **Matt Damon, actor**

Quay Grand

61 Macquarie Street, East Circular Quay
See index

Shangri-La Hotel

176 Cumberland Street, The Rocks
See index

The Park Hyatt

7 Hickson Road, The Rocks
See index

The Observatory Hotel

89–113 Kent Street, The Rocks
See index

The Sebel Pier One

Pier One, Hickson Road, The Rocks
See index

Hotel InterContinental

Cnr Bridge and Phillip Sts, Sydney
See index

Four Seasons Sydney

199 George Street, Sydney
See index

Sydney Harbour Marriott

30 Pitt Street, Sydney
See index

Restaurants, bars & pubs

Overseas Passenger Terminal

Circular Quay West, The Rocks

- **Cruise Bar and Restaurant** *Phone:* (02) 9251 1188
  Web: www.cruisebar.com.au
- **Ocean Room** See index
- **Wildfire** See index
- **Doyles at the Quay** See index
- **Quay** See index

Made of steel and glass, the Overseas Passenger Terminal (OPT) is the berthing place for some of the world's most luxurious cruise liners when they sail into Sydney Harbour between November and April. Cruise ships also depart from the OPT, but this isn't the only purpose of the terminal. It's also home to a number of the city's most spectacular high-end restaurants—**Wildfire, Ocean Room, Quay and Doyles at the Quay**—and **Cruise Bar**, a great bar which opens right onto the lower level of the OPT, giving patrons an eye-level perspective as Jet Cats and ferries pull into and depart from Circular Quay. The names of the venues on the upper two levels of the complex have changed over the years, but are never a bad spot for a drink or a bite to eat with stunning views. The Overseas Passenger Terminal has also been the HQ of Australian Fashion Week for many years when an influx of beautiful models and fashion types descend on the venue to see the collections of Australia's top designers showcased in April/May every year.

Aria

1 Macquarie Street Sydney
See index

Guillaume at Bennelong

Bennelong Point, Sydney
See index

Yoshii

115 Harrington Street, The Rocks
Phone: (02) 92472566 ***Web:*** www.yoshi.com.au
If you can't handle the six-month wait list at Tetsuya's (see index), you can still have a special Japanese dining experience in Sydney. There's no a la carte menu, just two impressive degustation menus.

'Here you can just let your tummy hang out and laugh out loud and not be on your guard. You don't have to self-edit ... sometimes in Los Angeles, if you're having a lot of business dinners, you have to be a bit more careful about what you say.' **Sarah Wynter, actor**

Altitude

Level 36, Shangri-La, 176 Cumberland Street, The Rocks
See index

Pony Lounge and Dining

The Rocks Centre, cnr Argyle and Playfair Sts, The Rocks

Phone: (02) 9252 7797 ***web:*** www.ponyrestaurant.com

This lounge and bar is tucked away on historic Kendall Lane, making it the perfect spot for an anonymous dinner for a big-time celeb.

Celeb Scoop: Check out this spot during Fashion Week—it's sure to be packed with models, and Australian designers.

Rockpool

107 George Street, The Rocks
See index

Cafe Sydney

Level 5, Customs House, 31 Alfred Street, The Rocks
See index

Opera Bar

Lower Concourse, Sydney Opera House,
Bennelong Point, Circular Quay

Phone: (02) 9247 1666 ***Web:*** www.operabar.com.au

Opera Bar's unbeatable outdoor waterside location is about as close to two of the city's biggest icons as you could get—adjacent to the Sydney Opera House and opposite the Sydney Harbour Bridge. A party place all week long, especially in summer.

Celeb Scoop: US singer Jesse McCartney was almost refused entry to this bar. Though he was under 21 and below the legal drinking age in the US, at the time Jesse was over 18, which is the legal drinking age in Australia. However, the bouncer was confused when reading Jesse's US driver's licence which lists your date of birth as month, date and year as opposed to the Australian standard of date, month and year.

Bridge Bar

Level 10, Opera Quays, Circular Quay

Phone: (02) 9252 6800

Suspended magnificently between two buildings, Bridge Bar combines stunning tenth-floor harbour and city views with an impressive line-up of specialty stick drinks. Beautiful views, and a place where celebs have been known to escape for a low key drink.

Celeb Scoop: Australian cricketing spin-bowler Stuart MacGill celebrated a seven-wicket haul and his wife Rachel Friend's birthday at Bridge Bar.

Uber Bar

Upstairs, The Lowenbrau Keller, cnr Argyle and Playfair Sts, The Rocks

Phone: (02) 9264 9188 *Web:* www.lowenbrau.com.au/uberbar.htm

An excellent live gig venue, this is also one of the best places in the city to sample a premium Munich Pure Bier downstairs at Sydney's most authentic Bavarian-style pub, The Lowenbrau Keller.

Celeb Scoop: Before he found fame in Oz, singer James Blunt performed his first Australian media showcase here in 2005.

Blu Horizon Bar

Level 36, Shangri-La Hotel, 136 Cumberland Street, The Rocks

Phone: (02) 9250 6000 *Web*: www.shangri-la.com

For 360-degree city and harbour views, head to the top of the Shangri-La Hotel. Behind the bar are some of the world's best bartenders serving up exotic cocktail concoctions.

Celeb Scoop: Channel Ten staged the twentieth anniversary party for *The Bold and The Beautiful* was held here in 2007, attended by cast members Ronn Moss, Katherine Kelly Lang, Mackenzie Mauzy and Kyle Lowder.

The Argyle

12-18 Argyle Street, The Rocks

Phone: (02) 9247 5500 *Web*: www.theargyle.biz

Named after a mythical beast, The Argyle opened its doors early in 2007 after a multimillion dollar transformation turned a bric-brac gallery (and formerly Sydney's very first Customs House) into one of the city's most impressive bar complexes. Spread over two floors, The Argyle has five bars including one in an old-world cobblestone courtyard and another on the top floor reserved for VIPs only that boasts a flowing lava bar.

Celeb Scoop: On the launch night, all the booths in the VIP Reiby Room were packed with famous faces: Alex Dimitriades, Zoe Naylor, Annelise Seubert and Jon Stevens. This A-list crew enjoyed unlimited rounds of Moet and The Argyle's signature club sandwiches at midnight.

The Palisade Hotel

35 Bettington Street, The Rocks

Phone: (02) 9247 2272 *Web:* www.palisadehotel.com

Established during World War I, this five-storey building stands alone in Millers Point, overlooking the harbour. Its heritage exterior makes it a popular backdrop for film locations. Many films including *Dirty Deeds, Return to Eden* and *The Matrix* were shot in the area using the Palisade as a backdrop. Stars John Goodman, Colin Friels, Hugo Weaving and Bryan Brown all enjoy the low-key atmosphere this pub offers and have frequented the bar. Up the steep stairs is a first-class restaurant where Sydney politicians and entrepreneurs like to dine. Keep on climbing and you reach the rooftop level, from where you will have unsurpassed views of the harbour. Or pop in for a lazy afternoon of cheap and cheerful food free of any city fuss.

Celeb Scoop: Kylie Minogue shot one of her video clips here, and *The Matrix* crew shot a scene here.

'I spent my whole 37th year in Sydney working on the Matrix *films. I just loved the city. Great people, beautiful weather, beautiful architecturally and there's good cuisine there.'* **Keanu Reeves, actor**

The Glenmore

96 Cumberland Street, The Rocks

Phone: (02) 9247 4794 *Web:* www.glenmorehotel.com

Patrons at the Glenmore Hotel in the 1950s may have wondered what the tall, lean, handsome man was sketching as he nursed his schnapps and stared into the distance. Turns out this was Jorn Utzon, who had just won a competition to design the new Sydney Opera House and found this pub gave him the best vantage point for his future masterpiece. Head straight up the narrow staircase and you will be on the rooftop, sharing Utzon's view. If it's raining, try the downstairs bar.

Celeb Scoop: Nicole Kidman and director Baz Luhrmann have been seen sitting at one of the back tables next to the windows in deep conversation. Former Australian cricket captain and now television cricket commentator Mark Taylor came in for a beer after a BridgeClimb. British-born actor and star of *In the Name of the Father,* Pete Postlethwaite, is a favourite celeb customer among bar staff because of his friendly nature.

The Australian Hotel

100 Cumberland Street, The Rocks

Phone: (02) 92472229 *Web:* www.australianheritagehotel.com

The winner of the Best Specialty Beer Award at the 2006 Bar Awards, the Australian Hotel is located in a quiet street at the top of The Rocks and has been a popular destination since the early 1800s (although the current pub was not built until 1913). Along with one of the most expansive beer lists, this old-style pub offers some of the city's most casual Australian cuisine. Gourmet pizzas are topped with

Australian produce—emu, crocodile, kangaroo and duck pizzas are specialties of the house.

> Celeb Scoop: UK acting great Pete Postlethwaite spent many afternoons here while performing in Australia in 2003. On her visit to Sydney in 2003 to promote *Charlie's Angels: Full Throttle*, Hollywood actor Drew Barrymore stopped by and ordered an emu pizza. Actor Paul Hogan staged his film premiere afterparty for *Crocodile Dundee in Los Angeles* here in 2001.

The Harbour View

18 Lower Fort Street, The Rocks

Phone: (02) 9252 4111 *Web:* www.harbourview.com.au

The Harbour View sits in the shadow of the Harbour Bridge and is a popular choice for Aussie celebs including cricketers Shane and Brett Lee, Mark Waugh and Michael Slater; TV stars like Tom Williams; musicians like Alex Lloyd; former Miss Universe Jennifer Hawkins; news reporters; swimming sensation Dawn Fraser; and the former prime minister Bob Hawke. The restaurant has incredible views of the Bridge and was a regular eating spot for British ice-skaters Jane Torville and Christopher Dean, when they're visiting Australian shores.

> Celeb Scoop: Famed ice skaters Jane Torville liked to order the fish of the day, while Christopher Dean is a fan of the fillet steak.

Theatre & music

Sydney Opera House

Bennelong Point, Circular Quay

See index

Sydney Theatre Company and the Wharf

Hickson Road, The Rocks

See index

'We have tried to live in a few other places, but something really hit us in the gut. It's just a feeling about what home is. It became clear to us that family and the theatrical community in Australia, in Sydney, were a large part of who we are.' **Cate Blanchett, actor**

The Dendy, Opera Quays

1–7 Macquarie Street, East Circular Quay

Phone: (02) 9247 3800 *Web:* www.dendy.com.au

It's almost a shame to even consider leaving the spectacular harbour views of East Circular Quay behind to enter a cinema, but the Dendy isn't your average movie house. Catering to a more cultured crowd, this Dendy is known for its arthouse playlist. It has also played host to some red-carpet film openings, and the who's who of the celebrity world have all popped up for a premiere at this prime harbour-front cinema. Heath Ledger and Naomi Watts appeared for the Australian opening of *21 Grams*, Toni Collette for *Connie and Carla*, and Sarah Wynter joined David Wenham for *Three Dollars*.

> Celeb Scoop: The gourmet choc-tops here have to be tasted to be believed. Go for the double choc or cherry ripe variety— they're sensational, as fashion designer Wayne Cooper will attest (he was tucking into one during the premiere of *21 Grams*).

'I love Sydney. There is an exhale here once I hit the ground. There is an ease here. I don't know if it's an Australian thing or if it's Sydney or the weather or the culture or just me feeling like, "OK, I'm back home", but it's definitely there.' **Sarah Wynter, actor**

The Basement

29 Reiby Pl, Circular Quay

Phone: (02) 9251 2797 *Web:* www.thebasement.com.au

The Basement has been a landmark of the Australian music scene since the early 1970s. Grab a meal and show here for around $30.

Jazz, blues, solo acoustic and more are on offer, and you might be lucky enough to see an incognito muso or two enjoying the show.

Celeb Scoop: Actress Toni Collette performed here after making her foray into the world of music, and Russell Crowe has also taken to the stage here with his band 30 Odd Foot of Grunts.

Galleries & museums
Museum of Contemporary Art (MCA)
140 Hickson Road, The Rocks
See index

Ken Done Gallery
1 Hickson Road, The Rocks
Phone: (02) 9247 2740 **Web:** www.kendone.com.au
Ken Done's artworks are distinctive and recognisable for their Australian references, so they make great souvenirs. As well as canvas artworks, Done produces books, clothing, accessories and homewares.

Celeb Scoop: Britney Spears caused a stir at Bondi beach wearing an itsy bitsy Ken Done polka dot bikini during her *Crossroads* movie tour in 2002.

Outdoor & adventure
Sydney Harbour Bridge and BridgeClimb
5 *Cumberland Street, The Rocks*
See index

'*BridgeClimb was amazing—you learn so much about the structure. Our instructor was amazing. Cameron [Diaz] and I had a great time.*' **Justin Timberlake, singer**

Royal Botanic Gardens

Mrs Macquaries Road, Sydney

Phone: (02) 9231 8111 *Web:* www.rbgsyd.nsw.gov.au

Wrapping around Farm Cove and adjoining the Sydney Opera House, Sydney's Royal Botanic Gardens are Australia's oldest gardens, established by Governor Macquarie in 1861. Stroll or run through the gardens and you might wind up exercising alongside a baseball-capped Matt Damon when he's in town promoting a new film project, or Russell Crowe, who lives in Farm Cove's neighbouring bay, Woolloomooloo in a luxury apartment he purchased for $8.25 million. At Mrs Macquarie's Chair, a stone viewing platform erected by convicts in the 1800s, you can catch a film at the Openair Cinema during the summer. Premieres are often held here, too, attracting the Sydney social set and local identities.

Celeb Scoop: In *The Matrix Revolution*, characters The Oracle and The Architect meet in the gardens for an important chat. Regular jogger Russell Crowe also appears here in a scene from *The Sum of Us*, a local film he made just before he became internationally famous. Jessica and Ashlee Simpson, and Matt Damon and his mother, have all cruised past this picturesque vantage point. Nicole Kidman and Tom Cruise spent New Year's Eve 1999 moored not far from Mrs Macquarie's Chair on James Packer's yacht, *Arctic P.*

Shopping
DFS Galleria

155 Hickson Road, The Rocks

Phone: 8243 8666 *Web:* www.dfsgalleria.com

Just a short walk from the heart of the CBD you'll find one of the city's largest duty-free shopping emporiums. This is a great place to pick up your duty-free bargains, particularly if you're a fan of luxury beauty brands.

Also on The A-list
Fitness First

20 Bond Street, Sydney

Phone: 1 300 55 77 99 ***Web:*** www.fitnessfirst.com.au

As of mid-2007, there were five Fitness First health clubs in the immediate vicinity of the CBD. State of the art gym equipment and the latest gym classes attract a body conscious clientele, from politicians to sportstars, actors and soapie stars.

Celeb Scoop: It's not only the high-flying business execs who sweat it out at the Bond Street gym—Will Smith trained here when he was in town with his wife Jada Pinkett Smith, who was filming *The Matrix*. *US Biggest Loser* trainer, Bob, also works out here when he is in Oz.

'*I love Sydney, it's just great. Jada and I did look at buying a place there.*' **Will Smith, actor**

City Central

'Whenever I'm not living here, it's like, "what am I doing living in America for, what am I doing?" I miss it when I'm not here. And I also miss the little things like the footy and eating pies and Paddle Pops.' **Simon Baker, actor**

Like major cities the world over, Sydney's CBD has become a hive of apartment buildings and bars and clubs, where celebrities, high-profile business types and international visitors flock to soak up some inner-city living. Living in the city has a cachet which attracts many big names.

Stretching from the edge of the Royal Botanic Gardens and the Domain in the east (see index) to King Street Wharf, Darling Harbour, Pyrmont and Ultimo in the west, the **CBD** is an array of multicultural gems.

Architecturally, the highlights of Sydney's retail map include the Queen Victoria Building and The Strand Arcade, which have retained their original Victorian architecture and, for the most part, the shops are upmarket and Australian.

Macquarie Street, once the Harley Street of Sydney, is lined with the clinics and practices of top specialist medicos (who are frequented by visiting celebs in emergencies). Sydney Hospital is also situated on this street, the square at the rear of which was the setting for *Babe: Pig In The City* (where Babe snuck through to free his friends).

Corporate businesses operate from some of the city's grandest buildings, alongside The State Library, New South Wales Parliament House, the former Royal Australian Mint and Hyde Park Barracks which all sit at this end of the city.

In the centre of the city is Martin Place, the core of Sydney's business quarter—home to the Colonial Centre (Elizabeth Street corner) which has a starring role in *The Matrix* in the scene where Laurence Fishburne's character is held captive before being

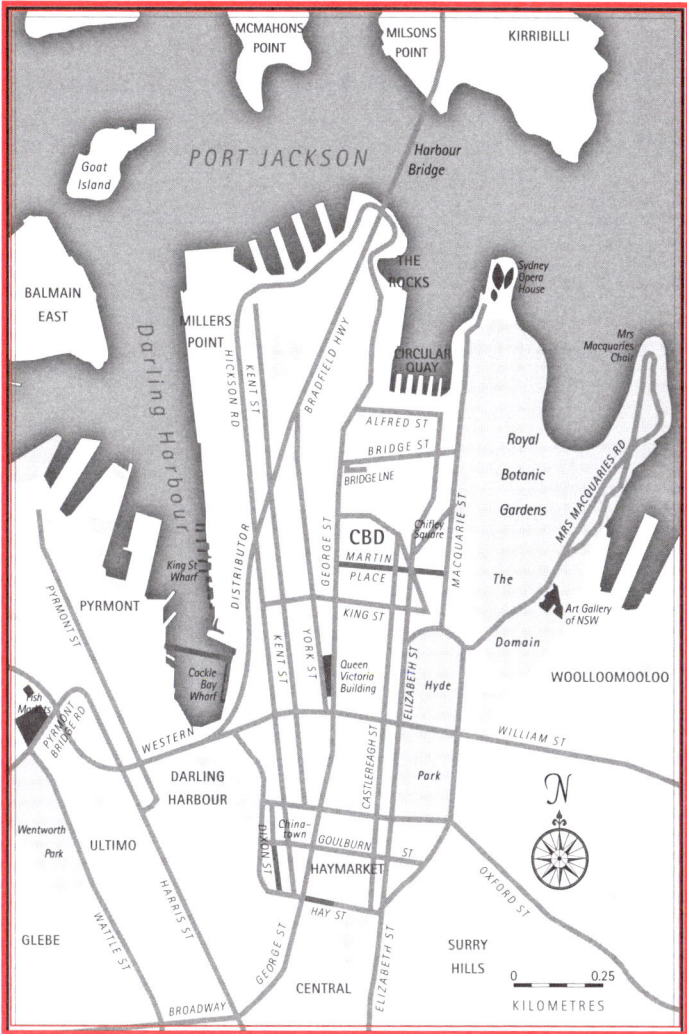

City Central

rescued by Keanu Reeves. Further down is the fountain that forms the background to the agent-training program and at the grand old colonial building—1 Martin Place—sits the staircase where Reeves experienced deja vu and saw the same black cat walk past twice.

But enough about movies. The revamped GPO Building in Martin Place is a visual feast, and is packed with some of Sydney's best restaurants and bars, including a basement food court modelled on the one in Harrods. The most glamorous place to be seen will be The Ivy in George Street. Set to open in 2007, it will be the latest entertainment masterpiece from society-magnates the Hemmes family.

Modern architectural highlights include Renzo Piano's Aurora Place in Macquarie Street, and Sydney Tower, the 305-metre pinnacle of the city.

The restaurant faves of the famous are dotted all over the city. Italian eatery Machiavelli on Clarence Street is regularly frequented by high-profile names of all shapes and sizes, from Kylie Minogue lunching with her mum, to Rupert Murdoch and the late Kerry Packer. Bilson's is one of the best in town for food and well-known diners, as is Glass, within the Sydney Hilton. On King Street Wharf, a cluster of upmarket restaurants and bars sit together, hosting many big names visiting or living in Sydney.

Like much of Sydney, the central locale is full of colourful contrasts. Australian model Megan Gale, who is the face of department store David Jones, regularly shops there. Nicole Kidman usually calls into David Jones when in town, often to shop at the Chanel cosmetics counter. Like any world-class city, Sydney has a strip that attracts the rich, the famous and those just wanting to see what all the fuss is about—you'll find it at the gold-gilded end of Castlereagh Street which is home to luxury brands including Gucci, Louis Vuitton and Cartier.

At the other end of the CBD is **Haymarket**, home to Sydney's Chinatown district, the Sydney Entertainment Centre, markets, bargain shopping galore, and places to shop, eat and drink.

Darling Harbour has gone through a series of reincarnations, as different restaurants and hotels have come and gone. Just across the bay, you'll find fresh, innovative and diverse dining experiences lining up along **King Street Wharf**. Residents live upstairs in apartments, and trendy offices sit above the array of restaurants overlooking the water.

Sydney's only casino, **Star City,** constantly attracts the big names— usually in the wee hours when the city's and DJs have stopped. Its surroundings in **Pyrmont** and **Ultimo** are low-key, but some of Sydney's elite have gravitated towards the classy apartments on the water's edge. The **Ian Thorpe Aquatic Centre** (cnr Harris and William Henry Streets) will be a welcome addition to the area. Named after Thorpey, the five-time gold medal winning champion, the centre cost $40 million and will be the largest aquatic centre in the CBD.

Hotels

Establishment Hotel

5 Bridge Lane, Sydney
See index

Sofitel Wentworth Hotel

61-101 Philip Street, Sydney
See index

The Hilton Sydney

488 George Street, Sydney
See index

Sheraton on the Park

161 Elizabeth Street, Sydney
See index

Medina Executive Sydney Central

2 Lee Street, Haymarket
See index

Restaurants, bars & pubs

The Establishment

252 George Street, Sydney

Phone: (02) 9240 3100 *Web:* merivale.com/establishment

This hotel and restaurant complex is up there with the best in the world, and if there was a Sydney 'It' boy, Establishment owner Justin Hemmes would be it. Opened in 2000, the Establishment building is a restored warehouse and includes Hemmesphere, one of Sydney's sexiest lounge bars, on the top floor, a hotel, the restaurant est., Tank Stream Bar, Tank nightclub, and The Garden Bar and Asian Kitchen.

Celeb Scoop: U2's Bono and members of Pearl Jam partied together at Hemmesphere to celebrate the US mid-term election results in November 2006. Jamiroquai front man Jay Kay spent time in the plush bar after concert tour performances, as did Brit bad boy Robbie Williams in 2004, though he preferred the Garden Bar on the hotel's ground level. Olympic swimmer Ian Thorpe is also a regular at Tank nightclub.

'I'm in the country for three weeks and I plan to shag myself silly—you just need to be there at the bar.' **Robbie Williams, singer**

The Ivy

320 George Street, Sydney

Web: www.merivale.com

The Hemmes family's latest venture (set to open late 2007) will be a super luxurious place for international stars to party and stay. Rumoured to have cost upwards of $50 million, The Ivy has been in the making for three years. At the time of going to print, The Ivy was set to feature a day spa, eight restaurants, a swimming pool with bar and dance floor, outdoor terraces and European-style laneways and shops. Two purpose-built party penthouses were also planned to occupy the top floors of the five-storey building, each staffed with its own cocktail bars, pool and spa.

Zeta Bar

Level 4, Hilton Sydney, 488 George Street, Sydney

Phone: (02) 9265 6070 *Web:* www.zetabar.com.au

Designed by New York's Tony Chi, Zeta Bar attracts a cool, city slicker crowd and a whole bunch of big international names who head straight for the red curtained-off booths.

Celeb Scoop: Snoop Dogg partied here behind curtains and had his minders invite beautiful women inside. When US gossip guru Perez Hilton came down with a bout of pneumonia in 2007, rather than cancel his party, a bed was set up inside the bar.

The Summit Restaurant & Orbit Lounge

Level 47, Australia Square, 264 George Street, Sydney

See index

Forty One Restaurant

2 Chifley Square, Sydney

See index

Machiavelli Ristorante Italiano

123 Clarence Street, Sydney

See index

Tetsuya's

529 Kent Street, Sydney

See index

Bambini Trust Cafe and Wine Bar

Street James Trust Building, 185 Elizabeth Street, Sydney

Phone: (02) 9283 7098 *Web:* www.bambinitrust.com.au

Plenty of celebrities have graced the tables here. Located next to the offices of the ACP magazine company, editors, writers and advertising execs all lunch here. It's regularly named as Sydney's best European style bar.

> Celeb Scoop: Close friend of Tom Cruise, James Packer, is often seen here. Everyone from Megan Gale to local TV stars have been here.

Civic Hotel

Cnr Pitt and Goulburn Streets, Sydney

Phone: (02) 8080 7000 *Web:* www.civichotel.com.au

Many icons of Aussie music got their start here in the 1970s, including INXS, Midnight Oil and Mental as Anything. Built in 1940, the grand Art Deco feel makes this a great spot for a drink, and the building is now heritage-listed. The food is some of the best in this part of town.

The Slip Inn

111 Sussex Street, Sydney

Phone: (02) 9240 3000 *Web:*www.merivale.com.au

A big hit with the CBD suits, this is another popular drinking venue in the Hemmes stable, where history has proven is fit for Princes and Princesses.

> Celeb Scoop: The al fresco area downstairs at the Slip Inn is where Mary met Frederik—as in Crown Princess Mary of Denmark. The two met here during the 2000 Sydney Olympic Games. The bar now features a special cocktail as a tribute to the royal couple's meeting.

Home Nightclub

The Promenade, Cockle Bay Wharf, Sydney

Phone: (02) 9266 0600 *Web:* www.homesydney.com

This popular Sydney nightspot often plays host to some of Sydney's well-known celebs. Up to 2000 people cram in on Saturday nights.

King Street Wharf

Funky bars and restaurants line this waterside strip on the city fringe.

- **Bungalow 8** *Phone:* (02) 9299 4660
  Web: www.bungalow8.com.au
  Not quite as good as its New York namesake, but a great party place especially in summer.
- **Cargo Bar and Lounge** *Phone:* (02) 9262 1733
  Web: www.cargobar.com.au
  This is *the* place to party during racing season.
- **Kobe Jones** *Phone:* (02) 9299 5290
  Web: www.kobejones.com.au
  Innovative Japanese Californian cuisine creations.

The Loft

Lime Street, King Street Wharf, Sydney

Phone: (02) 9299 4770 *Web:* www.theloftsydney.com

This is a hot location for after-parties during Fashion Week (see index) and for media launches. Foxtel threw *Sex and The City*'s Jason Lewis a party here when he was in town, Sarah O'Hare has hosted Breast Cancer Foundation parties and Daniel Johns, Paul Mac, Ronn Moss, Pete Murray and Duran Duran have all had a tipple here.

'I gotta tell you, I like this city a lot. New York is much more congested, there's more pressure and pace. I love New York, but there's a feeling of ease here.' Jason Lewis, actor

Chinatown

Great food, shopping and markets, all within a short walk from the centre of Sydney.

- **BBQ King** 18–20 Goulburn Street, Sydney
  Phone: (02) 9267 2586
  No-frills Chinese, with roast duck and pork to die for. Aussie rocker Jimmy Barnes has been seen tucking into a late night feast here.
- **East Ocean** Enter from 421–429 Sussex Street and 86–88 Dixon Street, Haymarket *Phone:* (02) 9212 4198
  Yum cha and Chinese food. Another spot where celebrity chefs can be seen after dark grabbing a bite, when their own restaurants have closed for the night.

Theatre, cinema & music
State Theatre

49 Market Street, Sydney

Phone: (02) 9373 6835 *Web:* www.statetheatre.com.au

This is a glittering homage to Art Deco Hollywood, and the beautifully ornate theatre continues to play host to some of the world's biggest film and musical names including Silverchair, Human Nature, Tom Cruise, Penelope Cruz, Renee Zellweger, Cameron Diaz, Antonio Banderas and Charlize Theron. One of the city's finest live performance venues and the closest thing Sydney has to Hollywood's Grauman's Chinese Theatre.

Celeb Scoop: At the premiere of *The Break-Up* in 2006, Jennifer Aniston and Vince Vaughn's introduction to the film for the 2000 plus audience of VIPs was like a stand-up comedy routine. Aniston appeared a little bit tipsy, and it was up to a quick-thinking Vaughn—her then beau—to save Aniston when she got confused by entertainment reporter Angela Bishop's none too probing questions about the film. At one stage the pair even launched into an impromptu karaoke style rendition of 'Islands in the Stream'.

Metro Theatre Sydney

624 George Street, Sydney

Phone: (02) 9550 3666 *Web:* www.metrotheatre.com.au

An intimate live music space, The Metro has had some huge acts take to the stage—from Russell Crowe and his band 30 Odd Foot of Grunts to Pink, Good Charlotte, Eskimo Joe and Keanu Reeves with his band Dogstar. A pivotal breakthrough venue for up and coming musos.

Celeb Scoop: Check out a live act here and you should keep your eyes on the crowd as well as the stage. The small, dim venue affords famous types the ability to blend into the crowd of music lovers.

'I love it, I just love Sydney. I always say that I want to visit as much as possible.' Joel Madden, Good Charlotte

Sydney Entertainment Centre

35 Harbour Street, Darling Harbour

Web: www.sydentcent.com.au

Music history has been made here. Bryan Adams, Powderfinger, Silverchair, Pink, Beyonce Knowles, Delta Goodrem, John Farnham, Usher, AC/DC, Backstreet Boys, Christina Aguilera are among some of the names to have played here. John Edward has even 'crossed over' for Australian audiences within the centre's walls. Kylie Minogue received a screaming ovation from her 11,000 fans when she toured here for the first time after battling breast cancer. Her costumes were designed by Karl Lagerfield, John Galliano and Dolce & Gabbana.

Celeb Scoop: Former Beatle George Harrison stunned audiences in 1984 when he stepped on stage and played with rock band Deep Purple during their concert tour here.

'This is the best venue in the world to play.' Sir Elton John

George Street Cinemas Entertainment Complex

505 George Street, Sydney

Phone: (02) 9273 7431 *Web:* www.greaterunion.com.au

The biggest cinema complex within the city itself is regularly used for Australian red carpet premieres when international stars and film-makers tour to promote their films. Rob Schneider, Jason Biggs, Seann William Scott, Naomi Watts, Heath Ledger, Russell Crowe and Mel Gibson are among the long list to have walked the carpet here. Premieres are listed at the front of the complex. Lining the red carpet is a sure-fire way to get a piccie with your favourite movie star.

Celeb Scoop: At the *School of Rock* premiere, Jack Black jumped onto the roof of the limousine he arrived in, jumped down onto the boot, jumped off, rolled down the red carpet and then curled up on the ground with his guitar.

'I've always been fascinated with Australia. It's the one place since I was a kid that I wanted to go. I was just so drawn to it and I had the most amazing experience. It put such a huge perspective, a different perspective, on my life.' **Seann William Scott, actor**

Imax Theatre

31 Wheat Road, Darling Harbour

Phone: (02) 9281 3300 *Web:* www.imax.com.au

IMAX is the super-large film format that gives you a larger-than-life movie experience. Ten times larger than the regular cinema format, these images are so real you'll think you were in the spectacular landscapes. The theatre screens films in 2D and 3D.

Galleries & museums

Art Gallery of New South Wales

Art Gallery Road, Sydney
See index

Museum of Sydney

Cnr Phillip and Bridge Sts, Sydney
See index

Powerhouse Museum

500 Harris Street, Ultimo
See index

Australian National Maritime Museum

2 Murray Street, Darling Harbour
See index

Outdoor & adventure

The Domain

Royal Botanic Gardens, Mrs Macquaries Road, Sydney

Phone: (02) 9231 8111 *Web:* www.rbgsyd.nsw.gov.au

Stretching from St Mary's Cathedral to the tip of Mrs Macquarie's Chair, the Domain is Sydney's answer to New York's Central Park, minus the zoo. Annual events include the Sydney Food and Wine Fair, the Australian music festivals Homebake (December) and Field Day (January), the world's largest short-film festival Tropfest (February) and Carols By Candlelight (December). The Domain also makes the perfect picnic and wedding photo location. A large car park is underground, perfect if you are driving into the CBD for a spot of city shopping.

Celeb Scoop: On the night prior to performing with her band The Finish at Homebake 2006 in front of 20,000 fans, Toni

Collette was so nervous she thought she was going to be sick. She overcame her stagefright and was sensational.

Hyde Park

Elizabeth Street, Sydney

This gorgeous city park plays host to many events throughout the year. At night, it is lit up with tiny magical lights in the trees.

Chinese Garden of Friendship

Darling Harbour (southern end)

Phone: (02) 9281 6863 *Web:* www.chinesegarden.com.au

Initiated by the local Chinese community to celebrate Australia's 1988 Bicentenary, the Chinese Garden is the result of a close bond of friendship and cooperation between the sister cities of Sydney and Guangzhou in Guangdong Province, China.

Shopping

Canturi Jewellery Salon

80 Castlereagh Street, Sydney

Phone: (02) 9231 1799 *Web:* www.canturi.com

A designer for Cartier in Paris for the past two decades, Stefano Canturi is a master in fine jewellery design. His flagship store on Sydney's Castlereagh Street showcases an array of his stunning and luxurious jewellery, including pieces which you may recognise from their big screen movie roles. International fame arrived when his designs scored a starring role in Baz Luhrmann's *Moulin Rouge*. The delicate 134-carat diamond and white gold necklace he made for Kidman's character, Satine, made the world pay attention and secured appearances for his jewels in *The Matrix* sequels, *Superman Returns* and on Melanie Griffith in *The Night We Called It A Day*.

Celeb Scoop: Naomi Campbell was one of the first big names to wear a Canturi creation—a simple Canturi diamond and white gold alphabet design N necklace. Oprah Winfrey has revealed she never removes her Canturi O—not even to shower—which was a gift from the jeweller himself.

Paspaley

Ground floor, 2 Martin Place, Sydney

Phone: (02) 9775 1000 ***Web:*** www.paspaley.com.au

Celebrities have been wearing Paspaley pearls since the company opened in the 1970s. The Martin Place store is a glamorous place in Sydney to purchase jewellery, and is worth a visit just to soak up the sheen. Their client list includes Tiffany & Co, David Yurman, Cartier and Harry Winston.

Giorgio Armani

4 Martin Place, Sydney

Phone: (02) 8233 5888 ***Web:*** www.armani.com

Some of the sexiest male stars have been suited up by this Euro designer. Good celeb spotting—especially during awards season.

Celeb Scoop: Ian Thorpe appeared here to do an instore signing for fans with copies of GQ *Australia* in 2000 which featured a special shoot of Ian by acclaimed photographer Herb Ritts.

Fairfax and Roberts

44 Martin Place, Sydney

Phone: (02) 9232 8511 ***Web:*** www.fairfaxandroberts.com.au

Beautiful Australian jewellery with an elegant, classic look is the feature of this beautiful store, which has been open since 1845, albeit in several locations around the city. The company has created some very private pieces passed down through generations of well-to-do Australian families, many of which are still kept in private collections.

Tiffany & Co.

28 Castlereagh Street, Sydney

Phone: (02) 9235 1777 ***Web:*** www.tiffany.com

With two levels of jewellery, don't leave without a signature blue box.

Gucci

MLC Centre, Castlereagh Street, Sydney

Phone: (02) 9232 7565 *Web:* www.gucci.com

Italian fashion and leathergoods label has a small but well-stocked store here, showcasing the latest wares.

Louis Vuitton

63 Castlereagh Street, Sydney

Phone: 1 300 883 880 *Web:* www.louisvuitton.com

Leather goods, shoes, stylish clothing, jewellery and eyewear are all in this gorgeous store, showcasing the best of French design and fashion.

Spencer and Rutherford

Elizabeth & Castlereagh Streets, Sydney

Web: www.spencerandrutherford.com

Larger than life accessories and matching luggage sets are staples of the A-list brigade so if you're in need of some, a purchase here will give you instant celeb cred.

Celeb Scoop: Tyra Banks and Princess Mary bought up big here. Princess Mary purchased a selection of ultra feminine accessories while Tyra was entranced by luggage in the Cafe Liqueur colourway and walked out with entire set!

David Jones

86–108 Castlereagh Street, Sydney

Phone: (02) 9266 5544 *Web:* www.davidjones.com.au

The two major department store chains in Australia are David Jones and Myer. Both compete for shoppers, celebrities to front their campaigns, and even designers to fill their floors. Tickets to the high-end biannual women's fashion season launches for both David Jones and Myer are highly sought after, with venues ranging from the Sydney Town Hall to theatres, and occasionally in the stores themselves.

French champagne, decadent nibbles and elegant gifts for all guests are usually on offer. Australia's premier designers are stocked over their multiple levels and Nicole Kidman is a regular shopper here for Chanel. The store also has a decadent food hall selling fresh produce and gourmet treats.

Celeb Scoop: Australian model Megan Gale—famous in Italy—has been the store's face for many years. She caused quite a stir in the windows of the department store, stopping traffic on Market Street when she appeared naked in a bathtub in the front windows to launch her bath and body range in 2005. Mandy Moore is a fan of the delicious milk and dark chocolate covered strawberries from the David Jones Food Hall.

Myer

436 George Street, Sydney

Phone: (02) 9238 9111 *Web:* www.myer.com.au

Sidney Myer arrived in Melbourne in 1899 as a penniless Russian immigrant and ended up creating one of the largest retail businesses in Australia. He and his brother worked briefly at a drapery store in Melbourne before moving to Bendigo, in country Victoria, where they opened the first Myer store in 1900. Melbourne was traditionally the homeland of Australian fashion and of Myer, but today the Sydney store is arguably Australia's best.

Celeb Scoop: Miss Universe winner Jennifer Hawkins is one of the store's faces, and Myer flew actor Mischa Barton out just to sit in the audience at the launch of a new fashion season. Paris Hilton shopped with friend Kim Kardashian at Myer in 2006. She visited her own perfume range, took a long look at herself in the mirror and spent hundreds of dollars on foundation, mascara, eye shadow, perfume and body lotion.

Strand Arcade

412-414 George Street, Sydney

Phone: (02) 9265 6855 *Web:* www.strandarcade.com.au

A gorgeous place for a leisurely wander, built in Victorian Sydney, this is the only arcade remaining today in its original form. Glamorous to the core, visiting celebrities of all shapes and sizes have shopped here. The Strand Arcade has three floors rising to a vaulted glass ceiling. Architecturally, it is one of the most beautiful places in the city to shop, and is packed with Australian designers, jewellers and unique, quality stores. On the upper levels you will find Australian designers such as Bettina Liano, Brave, Third Millennium, Alannah Hill, Bowie and Little Joe.

- **Strand Hatters** *Phone:* (02) 9231 6884
  Web: www.strandhatters.com.au
- **Alannah Hill** *Phone:* (02) 9221 1251
  Web: www.alannahhill.com.au
- **Bettina Liano** *Phone:* (02) 9223 3511
  Web: www.bettinaliano.com
- **Dinosaur Designs** *Phone:* (02) 9223 2953
  Web: www.dinosaurdesigns.com.au
- **Gary Castles** *Phone:* (02) 9232 6544
  Web: www.garycastlessydney.com
- **Bowie** *Phone:* (02) 9699 1188
  Web: www.bowie.com.au
- **Little Joe By Gail Elliott** *Phone:* (02) 9232 1997
- **Alex Perry** *Phone:* (02) 9233 6555
  Web: www.alexperry.com.au

Celeb Scoop: Fashion master Alex Perry is one of our most successful designers, here and abroad. Local and international names have worn Perry's designs, from Kate Ritchie and Jennifer Hawkins (who has a dress named after her in Perry's collection) to Eva Longoria and Jennifer Lopez. J.Lo's manager actually called Perry direct and had him fly dresses to Lopez for a concert tour. She ended up wearing two of the selections that Perry selected for her. Princess Mary, Jared Leto, Good Charlotte, Jesse McCartney and George Michael are all fans of Bowie's designs. Cindy Crawford spent time checking out Little Joe on her visit in 2007. Favoured by Naomi Watts, Sharon Stone, Helena Christensen, Ashley Judd and Elizabeth Hurley, the label was created by former model Gail Elliott who Cindy befriended on the catwalk in the 1980s and remains extremely close friends with.

Queen Victoria Building (QVB)

455 George Street, Sydney

Phone: (02) 9265 6855 *Web:* www.qvb.com.au

Completed in 1898, the QVB replaced the original Sydney markets, and is a Romanesque monument designed to resemble a Byzantine palace. Built as a monument to the long-reigning monarch Queen Victoria, construction took place in dire times, as Sydney was in a severe recession. It was totally revamped in the 1980s, and remains a classically elegant retail space.

- **Herringbone** *Phone:* (02) 9266 0500

  Web: www.herringbone.com.au

  The home of beautiful Australian-made shirts.

- **Oroton Shop** *Phone:* (02) 9261 1984

  Web: www.oroton.com.au

  Elegant Australian bags, purses and jewellery.

- **The ABC Shop** *Phone:* (02) 9286 3726

  Web: www.abc.net.au

  Books, DVDs and plenty of intelligent gifts, featuring all the best known Australian actors, musicians, artists and personalities.

Also on The A-list

Star City

80 Pyrmont Street, Pyrmont

Phone: (02) 9777 9000 ***Web:*** www.starcity.com.au

They don't call Sydney's waterside casino Star City for nothing. Many big time performers have visited Star City, including Kiss and Queen (who stayed in the hotel). The casino's high roller rooms recently underwent a massive refurbishment, increasing in size and upping the ante on their plush decor. These private inner sanctums remain some of the only places VIPs can still legally smoke in the city since the new smoking laws were introduced in 2007. As well as the gaming area, the casino has two theatres, great restaurants and bars, a hotel and a day spa, Star Spa, where treatment rooms have been named after legendary celebrities. The hotel features some super luxurious penthouses, complete with personal butler service able to fulfil unusual requests such as having swans in the baths. The rooftop pool and gym area is one of the best on offer in Sydney.

Celeb Scoop: Sportstars Lucas Neill, Dwight York, Shane Warne and singer Alex Lloyd have all tried their luck on the tables. Kerry Packer once famously tipped a waitress enough to pay off her mortgage. Super group Kiss have stayed at the hotel and used to walk around in full make-up. Craig David also tried to slip in incognito here wearing a beanie only to be told by security that he had to remove it as it broke the casino's dress policy. UK chefs Rick Stein and Ainsley Harriettt are big fans of Astral, Star City's only fine dining restaurant with 360° city and harbour views.

St Andrews Cathedral

Sydney Square, George Street, Sydney

Phone: (02) 9265 1661 ***Web:*** www.cathedral.sydney.anglican.asn.au

This beautiful cathedral was used to say goodbye to Michael Hutchence on November 22, 1997. One of Sydney's saddest and highest profile funerals, images of the celebrity-filled cathedral were broadcast around the world and the service was broadcast live within Australia as the music industry mourned the loss of one of its greatest sons. Hutchence's partner Paula Yates, former girlfriend Kylie Minogue, Tom Jones, Diana Ross and Nick Cave were just some of those who shed their tears.

Celeb Scoop: U2's Bono shared many special times with Hutchence in the South of France where the pair had neighbouring homes—he commissioned florist Susan Avery (see index) to make a gigantic traditional Irish claddagh ring for the funeral, making front page news around the world.

Sydney Aquarium

Sydney Aquarium Pier, Darling Harbour

Phone: (02) 8251 7800 *Web:* www.sydneyaquarium.com.au

Walk underwater and explore Australia's natural marine life.

Celeb Scoop: On their promo trip to Oz in 2006, the privacy of the Aquarium appealed to Jennifer Aniston and Vince Vaughn who were as busy canoodling as they were checking out marine life.

Sydney Fish Markets

Cnr Bank Street & Pyrmont Bridge Road, Pyrmont

Phone: (02) 9004 1100 *Web:* www.sydneyfishmarket.com.au

You'll catch more than fresh fish at Sydney Fish Markets. You're likely to catch a big name celeb, especially if they're an Aussie. This is the largest market of its kind in the southern hemisphere and the world's second largest seafood market in terms of variety outside of Japan.

Celeb Scoop: Christmas time is a good time to catch a celeb here. Russell Crowe always makes a trip at 2am on the 36-hour trade before Christmas, as do the Kidmans, when they're in town for the holidays. Dawn Fraser, Darren Beadman, Andrew Denton and Collette Dinnigan also shop here. Kerry Packer used to send his PA to collect his order.

Sydney Wildife World

Sydney Aquarium Pier, Darling Harbour

Phone: (02) 9333 9288 *Web:* www.sydneywildlifeworld.com.au

Sydney Wildlife World is home to a huge variety of Australian flora and fauna, and is easily accessible in the heart of Darling Harbour. Over 6000 animals live here in nine natural habitats and ecosystems.

Celeb Scoop: Actor and comedian Billy Crystal visited here on his February 2007 trip to Sydney.

'Hopefully we can all come back on vacation next year. Both my kids are into Australian wildlife. It would be great to spend time here with them.' **Cindy Crawford, model**

Simon Johnson

181 Harris Street, Pyrmont

Phone: (02) 9552 2522 *Web:* www.simonjohnson.com.au

See index

Pure Platinum

252 Pitt Street, Sydney

Phone: (02) 9267 4454 *Web:* www.pureplatinum.com.au

Table dancers and showgirls are alive and well in the heart of the CBD and this seems to be on of the more popular gentlemens' clubs, at least with American celebs. The venue was used for the premiere afterparty of *Deuce Bigalo: European Gigolo* in 2005 with the film's title star and funny man Rob Schneider even partaking in a spot of pole dancing.

Celeb Scoop: This strip club was one of the first ports of call for *Full House* and *E.R.* actor John Stamos in 2007. Stamos popped in the day after arriving from the States, signing autographs on the club's PP Dollars, which are used to tip the dancers by the clientele. Stamos even signed the door girl's arm!

Woolloomooloo

'I stay at the W Hotel [now Blue Hotel] in Woolloomooloo, down by this really cool finger wharf. There are boats and water and it's really peaceful. I stay in this loft room that's got the bedroom up in the balcony overlooking the main room. It's kind of funky but not too posh, not too over-the-top.'
Natalie Imbruglia, singer/songwriter

Once associated with seedy backpacker hostels, public housing estates, sailors ready to let loose after months at sea, the destitute and homeless, and prostitutes from the red-light district of Kings Cross, **Woolloomooloo**—Sydney's oldest suburb—has shaken off its shady reputation and is now considered a funky, edgy and somewhat exclusive hub. Most of its image makeover is thanks to a 1990s multi-million-dollar redevelopment of the historic Cowper Wharf, which was once used as the city's main shipping port.

When it comes to celebrity pull, Russell Crowe is the area's biggest claim to fame. The actor took up residence in a luxury pad at the northernmost point of the pier and, having been given Crowe's star stamp of approval, lavish five-star restaurants began to emerge, delivering a new calibre of clientele to the area. A hit with media moguls and identities, actors, agents, musicians and models—pretty much anyone who works in the entertainment and media business—Woolloomooloo is appreciated by these types for both its closeness and its distance from the hustle and bustle of the CBD. Its waterside location also means that celebs can arrive by boat to avoid paparazzi, and come as close as possible to rediscovering their lost anonymity. Hugh Jackman is often seen here when in town, usually with his wife and two children.

For lovers of five-star delights, there is only one real accommodation option at Woolloomooloo where you can experience

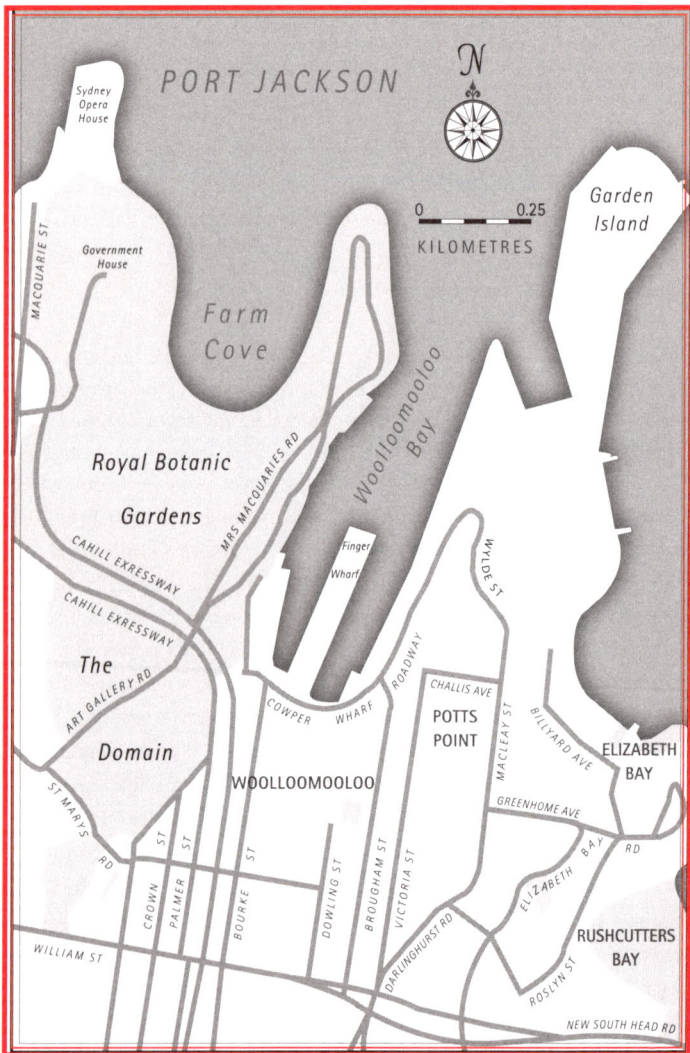

Woolloomooloo

the ultimate in celeb treatment—Blue Sydney (formerly the W Hotel)—and it is the jewel in the crown of what the Woolloomooloo area has to offer on the celebrity front. The hotel guest list reads like a Yellow Pages to the entertainment world—everyone from *2 Fast 2 Furious* star Paul Walker to multi-talented megastar Toni Collette—and its also been the location of many exclusive parties and premiere after-parties. *The Fantastic 4: Rise of the Silver Surfer* stars—including Jessica Alba and Julian McMahon—all celebrated here during the promotion of the comic book film adaptation.

Taking up the front half of the refurbished wharf, the hotel is also the portal for the many dining options located within the area, as they all line the city-facing exterior of the pier. The more high-end restaurant options are limited to those lining the wharf, and their first-rate nature and tucked-away location makes them prime celebrity territory. Otto is always a celebrity certainty—it's a favourite with everyone from Naomi Watts to Megan Gale and John Laws. There are also other casual eateries located just a short walk from the Cowper Wharf, including the Woolloomooloo Bay Hotel, Sienna Marina, the Tilbury Hotel and Pamela Anderson's favourite fast-food spot, the legendary Harry's Cafe de Wheels.

The other place of interest in the area is the Woolloomooloo Naval Base where international navy fleets routinely come into port.

Hotels
Blue Sydney
Cowper Wharf, 6 Cowper Wharf Road, Woolloomooloo
See index

Restaurants, bars & pubs
Cowper Wharf Restaurant Strip
Cowper Wharf, Cowper Wharf Road, Woolloomooloo
See index

Water Bar

Blue Sydney, Cowper Wharf, Cowper Wharf Road, Woolloomooloo

Phone: (02) 9331 9000 ***Web:*** www.tajhotels.com

Dark and intimate, the limited lighting of this bar is reminisce of Batman's Gotham City, though you're much more likely to meet the gaze of someone like Russell Crowe than Bruce Wayne. Crowe drinks here regularly, and in his wilder days was often politely told by management that it was time to go home. Sink into one of the leather booths or ottomans, perhaps alongside Heather Graham, Billy Idol or Natalie Imbruglia, and it's easy to lose track of time, especially if you sample some of the bar's signature cocktails, such as the Vanilla Passion, a favourite order of actress Jessica Alba.

Celeb Scoop: Usher and Jamie Foxx did shooters here together at the 2Day FM Star Party which Pink headlined. Wharf resident Russell Crowe has received the 'No more drinks' call on more than one occasion from bar management here.

'My manager is going to spend a lot of time with me on the Australian tour because he loves Australia. We've got a lot of friends there.' Pink, singer

The Tilbury Hotel

12–18 Nicholson Street, Woolloomooloo

Phone: (02) 9368 1041 ***Web:*** www.tilburyhotel.com.au

Refurbished in 2002, the hotel has a funky and intimate atmosphere, with a great cocktail lounge and outdoor area upstairs. The dining room downstairs has a modern Italian menu that changes daily. If you can, sample the yabbies, a favourite of Cannes Film Festival award-winner, Gregor Jordan—the film-maker who discovered Heath Ledger.

Celeb Scoop: Popular Aussie TV actress Georgie Parker got her big break at the Tilbury 20 years ago, belting out 'Georgie Girl' as part of a Seekers revue, four shows every weekend. She remembers being ignored by her audience of drunk sailors and girls on hen's nights: 'One night [the hen's night girls] all had little clockwork penises jumping all over the tables', she reminisces. 'I remember thinking this is the hardest gig I'll ever have'.

The Woolloomooloo Bay Hotel

2 Bourke Street, Woolloomooloo

Phone: (02) 9357 1177

Rebranded and revamped in early 2006, this iconic hotel is an institution among naval officers who come into port. The fact that it is low-key appeals to celebrities like area resident Russell Crowe who is a regular patron.

Celeb Scoop: Getting a taxi can be a nightmare on Melbourne Cup Day, even in Sydney, they don't call it the race that stops a nation for nothing! That's probably why Russ stayed close to home one Melbourne Cup Day and watched the race here.

Sienna Marina

67-41 Cowper Wharf Road, Woolloomooloo

Phone: (02) 9358 6299 *Web*: www.siennamarina.com.au

Though the wharf's fine dining restaurants are always bound to have a famous face dining within them, on the odd occasion, this charming eatery directly across from Blue Sydney is a good place to catch one.

Celeb Scoop: Russell Crowe uses this restaurant to host business meetings from time to time. In June 2007, Crowe met with his business associates Bra Boy Sunny Abberton (brother of surfer Koby), and director Phillip Noyce. Crowe was feeling particularly generous on this occasion, sending a bottle of St Hugos 2003 Cab Sav to a photographer nearby.

Harry's Cafe de Wheels

Cowper Wharf, Cowper Wharf Road, Woolloomooloo
See index

'*There are a number of great places to eat in the city, especially on the wharf at Woolloomooloo ... Then there's the landmark, Harry's Cafe de Wheels. Meat is a huge thing in Australia so you go there for a meat pie.*' **Naomi Watts, actor**

Also on The A-list
Spa Chakra

Cowper Wharf, Cowper Wharf Road, Woolloomooloo
Phone: (02) 9368 0888 *Web:* www.spachakra.com
The only spa centre in the Woolloomooloo area, Spa Chakra is located inside the Blue Hotel. Many celebs have robed (and disrobed) inside the treatment rooms of Spa Chakra, one of the first fully integrated medi-spas to launch in Australia.

Celeb Scoop: With names like Nicollette Sheridan, Jessica Alba and Toni Collette all having stayed at Blue Sydney—and with Russell Crowe's wife Danielle Spencer a resident on the wharf, it's pretty likely you'll spot a star here if you check in for some A-list treatment.

East Sydney, Darlinghurst & Surry Hills

'*You can do absolutely anything in the city, from climbing the Bridge to going to one of my favourite places, the restaurant row in Crown Street, Surry Hills.*' Michellie Jones, triathlete

This is the area that a sea of the city's artisan and theatrical crowd—including actors, musicians and film-makers—call 'home sweet home'. Borders and boundaries of where each suburb begins and ends are blurred, just as the way the cool and eclectic offerings of the localities blend in with pockets of uber cool sophistication.

Affectionately known as 'Darlo' by local residents, **Darlinghurst**, is very much about being understated rather then showy. The atmosphere is relaxed and laidback, making it a popular spot on weekends. The key look on the street verges from vintage glam to scruffy. Anything goes, though, which is why many celebrities like hanging out here, with many international stars discovering home-away-from-home hangouts during their visits.

One of the city's most cosmopolitan areas, there is something to suit everyone from every walk of life in Sydney's eastern realms—history, buzzing cafes and restaurants, one-off boutiques, second-hand and vintage clothing stores, restaurants, bars and nightlife. Not far from the trademark neon Coke sign in Kings Cross is Victoria Street, Darlinghust, a long stretch dotted with happening bars and restaurants. In any one of these restaurants, from Japanese to Thai to the authentic German schnitzels at Una's, it's not unheard of to bump into a filmmaking type of some sort, and Russell Crowe is a regular visitor.

The area is the home of film-maker Baz Luhrmann, actor Hugo Weaving and John Polson's internationally renowned short film

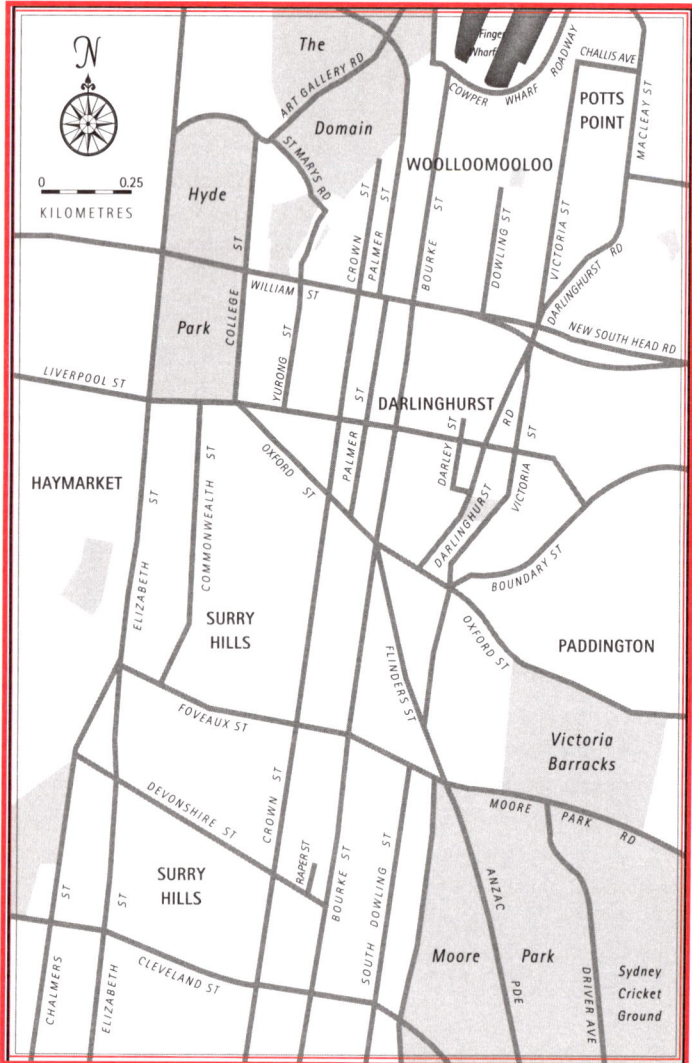

East Sydney, Darlinghurst & Surry Hills

festival, TropFest, as well as the Tropicana Caffe, where the festival got its humble beginnings. Actor/writer Joel Edgerton and his director brother Nash are also 'Darlo' residents, running their production company Blue Tongue Films from an office on Darlinghurst Road (number 249) for many years, not far from the art college (Burton Street) and the Harry Seidler-designed Horizon Apartments (Forbes Street), containing a penthouse worth over $15 million, along with apartments which are home to many of Sydney's actors, designers and local celebs.

Surry Hills has blossomed from a once depressed inner city area to a bustling, fashionable hub. Alternative fashion and vintage shops like Grandma Takes a Trip, CC's Flashback, Zoo Emporium and Nu + Naan on Crown Street attract savvy fashionistas, while the huge variety of its dining and pub strips, and in neighbouring **Waterloo** in the Danks Street precinct, ensures that the area is always alive—well, at least until the midnight curfew kicks in. Bar Cleveland and the Crown Hotel are the only hotels open past midnight.

One of the area's most famous residents has been singer Tim Finn of Crowded House fame, but you can catch many well-known Australian identities, especially of the TV and radio kind, buying their essentials at the local Surry Hills Shopping Village on Baptist Street. Famed Australian artist Brett Whiteley also ran his studio on Raper Street, which is now open to the public and exhibits a gallery of his most famous works. Not far away, boxer Anthony Mundine's gym is hidden upstairs behind a heavily graffitied doorway on **Redfern**'s Vine Street.

The title of 'Sydney's Restaurant Row' rightly belongs to Surry Hills and the seemingly endless road of eateries and pubs that make up Crown Street. Hugh Jackman's been seen having breakfast with his family at Bird Cow Fish at a table next to Naomi Watts; Megan Gale has bought her sushi at Matsuri; Olympic swimming great Ian Thorpe has enjoyed a drink at the Dophin Hotel; while *Neighbours* and *The Bill* star Daniel MacPherson used to frequent the Clock Hotel. While in town filming *Superman Returns*, Kate Bosworth was almost a daily patron at

Kawa on Crown Street. The street also has a few great lifestyle stores dispersed along it, including Vivid and Antikt—the place to pick up an exquisite furniture piece, mirror, painting or antique photo frame.

In Bourke Street and the surrounding streets, you'll find so many big sunnies and designer jeans packed into this seemingly endless cafe promenade, you'll be hard-pressed sorting the celebs from the wannabes. No matter—pop into any one of the cafes from and you'll feel like a VIP with their simple but tasty five-star cafe creations. While you're there, check out one of the many funky fashion boutiques like Mr Stinky and Mushu.

The adjacent neighbourhood of **East Sydney** is also home to some great eateries within easy walking distance of the CBD. Stanley Street is Sydney's 'other' little Italy, the first being the Leichhardt and Haberfield area in the city's inner west. Many celebs have been seen dining here, one of the most high profile being U2s Bono, who has enjoyed pizza in the area.

Hotels

Kirketon Hotel

229 Darlinghurst Road, Darlinghurst

Phone 1800 332 920 or (02) 9332 2011 *Web:* www.kirketon.com.au The first guests checked into this now luxury boutique hotel in the 1930s, but it was only in the late 1990s, when the hotel underwent massive renovations, that it earned itself the label as Darlinghurst's hippest hotel. Housing 40 stylish rooms—from standard to executive-style—a night here lets you unwind with a soak in a bath (a Villeroy & Boch bath suite, no less) with a deliciously scented passionfruit soap and then snuggle up in bed with your lamb's wool blanket.

Celeb Scoop: Ewan McGregor is one of the most famous guests to have stayed here.

Medina on Crown

359 Crown Street, Surry Hills

Phone: (02) 8302 1000 ***Web:*** www.medina.com.au

Because of its close proximity to some of the live venues in the area, this hotel is regularly used by record companies to put up visiting musos and rock bands.

Celeb Scoop: Ralph Fiennes held a party at a Surry Hills penthouse—believed to be at Medina—in January 2007, just before he joined the mile high club with Qantas airline stewardess Lisa Robertson. Loaded with top-shelf liquor, he and his guests partied hard until after 5 am.

Restaurants, bars & pubs
Tropicana Caffe

227 Victoria Street, Darlinghurst

Phone: (02) 9360 9809 ***Web:*** www.tropicanacaffe.com

The birthplace of the now world-recognised TropFest Film Festival in 1993, actors and creative types have always had a strong allegiance with the Tropicana. So popular did the exposure from the festival make the cafe, in 1996 its owners were able to double its size—then move to new premises on the other side of Victoria Street in 2001. Still, the food continues to be cheap, tasty and hearty, which explains why even today it remains popular with struggling arty types. Each year, Tropicana remains among the venues that screen the 12 TropFest competition finalists and the cafe has a strong commitment to helping the Sydney Children's Hospital.

Celeb Scoop: The who's who of the film industry flock to this short film festival birthplace, including Joel Edgerton, Keanu Reeves, who is a regular when in town and TropFest founder John Polsen.

'There are times when I spend hardly any time in Sydney but I will not say I live anywhere else. I've got my place in Sydney and whenever I'm not working, I'm here.' **Joel Edgerton, actor**

Kell's Restaurant & Bar

Kirketon Hotel, 229 Darlinghurst Road, Darlinghurst

Phone: (02) 9332 2011 *Web:* www.kirketon.com.au

Formerly Fix, the Kirketon's restaurant has been taken over by brothers Grant and Spencer Kells, who bring their international culinary experiences to this modern Australian/Asian inspired restaurant and bar.

Celeb Scoop: In its Fix days, *Good Charlotte*'s Benji Madden celebrated his girlfriend Sophie Monk's twenty-seventh birthday in this restaurant/bar's funky, intimate surrounds.

Bar Coluzzi

322 Victoria Street, Darlinghurst

Phone: (02) 9380 5420

First established on nearby William Street in the 1950s, this espresso bar and cafe introduced Sydneysiders to caffeine. The tiny, long serving cafe is one of the most popular spots on the Victoria Street strip.

Celeb scoop: Pull up a crate out the front here for a high quality coffee fix and you could see any number of actors, directors and film crew. Russell Crowe is a regular.

The Victoria Room

Level 1, 235 Victoria Street, Darlinghurst

Phone: (02) 9357 4488 *Web:* www.thevictoriaroom.com

Leather lounges mix with antique chairs and settees in this old-world, Victoriana-influenced sanctuary where you never know who you might bump into. The food is lush—especially the desserts—and there's also high tea on Saturdays between 4 pm and 6 pm.

The Green Park

360 Victoria Street, Darlinghurst

Phone: (02) 9380 5311

Situated on Victoria Street close to Darlinghurst's popular eateries
Una's and Phamish, the Green Park is a traditional, low-key, old-style
pub that attracts as many local residents as it does international
celebs. Pop in for a game of pool and a local beer and you might find
yourself engaged in conversation with a film-maker or actor.

Celeb Scoop: Actor Brandon Routh and director Bryan Singer
were regular patrons at the Green Park during their time in
Sydney filming *Superman*. In an effort to maintain their anonymity,
the pair spun one punter an interesting yarn: pretending to be
photographers on a global assignment snapping the sky!

'*Nothing beats—after a hard week at the TropFest office—going to
the Green Park and talking crap with more film-makers.*'
John Polson, actor and director, TropFest

Lo Studio

Upper ground floor, 53-55 Brisbane Street, Surry Hills

Phone: (02) 9212 4118 *Web:* www.lostudio.com.au

Housed in what was once the Paramount Pictures film studio,
the casting couches have given way to decadent chocolate hued
banquettes in this gorgeously slick Italian dining spot. Pristine white
walls are offset with marble floors and wood panelling—the perfect
contemporary feel for media moguls and lunching ladies of the press.

La Sala

Ground Floor, 23 Foster Street, Surry Hills

Web: www.lasala.com.au

A favourite of Sydney's media set, opened by Andrea Mellis in 2006, the dining room evokes memories of US Wolfgang Puk's deep set theatre-style dining rooms, and open kitchens. The Italian food is outstanding, and the broad wine list, appealing. Models Megan Gale and Jennifer Hawkins are just two well-known regulars.

Longrain

85 Commonwealth Street, Surry Hills

See index

Bentley Restaurant and Bar

320 Crown Street, Surry Hills

Phone: (02) 9332 2344 *Web:* www.thebentley.com.au

The team behind this New York-feeling bar love a good wine list ... this one features over 300 of the finest old and new world wines. They also serve some very tasty, unique tapas creations, and the cinnamon donuts for dessert are a must.

Celeb Scoop: The proprietors' previous establishment Moog (now closed) used to be a fave of Kylie Minogue's, who even swam in the pool attached to the bar/restaurant cum hotel, so we're sure she'll pop into this hot new venture to compare.

Billy Kwong

335 Crown Street, Surry Hills

Phone: (02) 9332 3300

Popular with foodies because of its association with celebrity chef and owner Kylie Kwong, this cosy modern restaurant puts a new spin on the traditional Shanghai tea house. Small, but never with enough tables to meet diners' demands, Kwong's signature dish is crispy skin duck with fresh blood-orange sauce. Her wagyu beef is mouthwateringly good—not suprising, after all she is a graduate of Neil Perry's Rockpool restaurant (see index). There's a no-booking policy in place here, but the oriental-inspired dishes (made only from organic produce) are definitely worth the lengthy wait. Besides, the Dolphin Hotel and some pre-dinner drinks are just across the road.

Celeb Scoop: In 2005, Kylie Kwong's ABC TV series *Heart and Soul* was filmed here. Well and truly one of the city's celebrity chefs, Kwong was so successful with her show that the *Heart and Soul* cookbook was one of the top-selling cookbooks in Australia for 2005.

Bills Surry Hills

359 Crown Street, Surry Hills

Phone: (02) 9360 4762 *Web:* www.bills.com.au

Established by famed Sydney chef, author and restaurant proprieter Bill Granger, this is one of several dining establishments operating under the 'Bills' name in Sydney. Located on the ground level of Medina Apartments, many a rock star can be seen enjoying a late brekky at this Surry Hills institution, thanks to the hotel's association with Sydney's record companies.

Celeb Scoop: Cameron Diaz goes here for breakfast every time she is in Sydney. Australian TV funnyman Rove McManus is a patron when he's in Sydney, as is Dannii Minogue, who has been spotted catching up with girlfriends and getting a caffeine fix here. Kate Bosworth is a big fan of the scrambled eggs.

Dolphin on Crown Hotel

412 Crown Street, Surry Hills

Phone: (02) 9331 4800 *Web:* www.dolphinhotel.com.au

After an impressive multi-million dollar refurbishment in 2005, the Dolphin Hotel became a popular hangout for cool Surry Hills locals. Artists, actors, musos, media types and sporting stars have all popped in for a beverage on the outdoor terrace or a Sunday roast from the hotel's kitchen.

Kawa

348a Crown Street, Surry Hills

Phone: (02) 9331 6811

All-day breakfast menus always go down well in Sydney and the one on offer at this trendy shabby-chic cafe is top quality. With fresh juices, organic and homemade items available, it's no surprise that brunch-loving Kate Bosworth visited this HQ of health almost daily when she was in town filming *Superman Returns*. If you read any interviews with Kate about her time in Sydney, she's guaranteed to mention Kawa: she gushes about the eatery so much you would think she is getting cafe kickbacks!

Celeb Scoop: Kate Bosworth's regular order was a freshly squeezed juice and one of their fresh baked breads.

'*The first place I went to is one of my favourite restaurants in Sydney—it's a little cafe on Crown Street called Kawa. I ended up going there pretty much every day.*' **Kate Bosworth, actor**

Cafe Mint

579 Crown Street, Surry Hills

Phone: (02) 9319 0848 *Web:* www.cafemint.com.au

Think of your ideal cafe. Now, with that vision in mind, head to Mint and you'll be amazed to discover that a café with perfect booth seating and amazing, *real* chai latte really does exist.

Pizza e Birra

Shop 1, 500 Crown Street, Surry Hills
Phone: (02) 9332 2510
This beer and pizza joint is one of the best in town, (and offers plenty of other authentic Italian dishes). The flour is flown in from Italy, as are many of the Italian wines on offer. There is a no-bookings policy, but it's worth the wait, as many celebs have discovered.

Celeb Scoop: Media mogul Lachlan Murdoch booked out the entire restaurant for his wife Sarah's thirty-fifth birthday in 2007. The windows were blacked out, and images of Sarah at various stages in her life were plastered on the walls. Guests included fashion designer Collette Dinnigan.

Sushi Suma

421 Cleveland Street, Surry Hills
Phone: (02) 9698 8873
One of Surry Hills's best-kept secrets, this Japanese-food lover's paradise is seriously good, as the queues out the front will always attest. The seafood is so fresh and the sashimi dishes are probably better than you'd get in Japan.

Bar Cleveland

Cnr Bourke and Cleveland Sts, Surry Hills
Phone: (02) 9698 1908 *Web:* www.barcleveland.com.au
A traditional old-style pub all the way, don't let its worn downstairs area put you off. Many celebs have popped in here for a beverage or two. Actor Sam Worthington has been spotted here knocking back a few ales.

Celeb Scoop: The wrap party for season three of Australian drama series *Love My Way* was held at this unassuming pub in February 2006. Its entire cast was present, including Ben Mendelsohn, Claudia Karvan and Brendan Cowell.

Cafe Zoe

688 Bourke Street, Surry Hills

Phone: 8399 0940

Media types, PR princesses and film stars come together in this well known Surry Hills cafe. Reportedly, this cafe was one of four in the area named after the original owner's sister but this is the only one still operated by the family of the initial operator. The food and service here is so good and well-received by its patrons they don't need to open on Sundays or over the Christmas break. The meatball spaghetti and homemade banana bread are hard to beat. Be on the lookout for emerging and established film-makers and actors, along with TV, sport and radio personalities who reside in the area.

Il Baretto

496 Bourke Street, Surry Hills

Phone: (02) 9361 6163

A favourite haunt of Surry Hills locals, this spot is about as basic as you can get for a meal, but the authentic Italian cuisine here is second to none. You can't book, but the pub across the road is a great place for pre-dinner drinks.

Celeb Scoop: Sydney identities Will Osmond of Will and Toby's fame and local TV face Kate Fischer often pop into this little local.

Cafe Niki

544 Bourke Street, Surry Hills

Phone: (02) 9319 7517 *Web:* www.cafeniki.com.au

One of the best—if not the best—cafes in the area, Cafe Niki is great for breakfast, brunch, lunch, afternoon tea or dinner. The outdoor courtyard is quaint and offers more privacy, but the booths and tables inside are super cosy—you'll feel right at home, especially once you sample their menu. Those with a sweet tooth will be unable to resist the French toast with caramelised banana and maple syrup—yum!

The Book Kitchen

255 Devonshire Street, Surry Hills 2010

Phone: (02) 9310 1003 *Web:* www.thebookkitchen.com.au

Simple, clean, organic, healthy gourmet food in a casual, relaxed local restaurant with reasonable prices is a formula which packs this restaurant all day on weekends. The dining area is filled with a large book case full of cookbooks from all corners of the globe. The trendy set love it, just be prepared to wait for a table.

Celeb Scoop: Actor Hugo Weaving is a regular here for his macchiato and breakfast, as are Lachlan and Sarah Murdoch. French chef Damien Puignolet is just one chef who called in here for lunch and signed his books (all for sale) on the spot.

Bourke Street Bakery

633 Bourke Street, Surry Hills

Phone: (02) 9699 1011

This place is legendary and it's not unusual to find a queue of customers winding around the corner onto Devonshire Street in order to sample the sought-after French-style wares of this bakery. Worth the wait, just as the cupcakes of New York's Magnolia Bakery are, so order up big when you get to the counter.

Celeb Scoop: Actor Hugo Weaving has been seen queuing up for the French sourdough sticks here.

Artisan Foccaceria

Cnr Liverpool and Palmer Streets, East Sydney

Phone: (02) 9326 9227 *Web:* www.artisans.com.au

Owned and operated by Sydney brother-and-sister duo Sam and Catherine Sgambellone, one of the four couples from the first series of TV reality program *My Restaurant Rules*, Artisan Foccaceria serves up delicious home-style Italian fare along with traditional cafè breakfast combos. Don't miss their divine brekkies, and the special highlight is their vanilla rice pudding with banana.

Stanley Street

- **Bill & Tony's** 74 Stanley Street, East Sydney
  Phone: (02) 9360 4702
- **Beppi's Restaurant** Cnr Stanley & Yurong Sts, East Sydney
  Phone: (02) 9360 4558 *Web:* www.beppis.com.au
- **Lord Roberts Hotel** 64 Stanley Street, East Sydney
  Phone: (02) 9331 1326 *Web:* www.lordrobertshotel.com.au
- **Pello** 71-73 Stanley Street, East Sydney
  Phone: (02) 9360 4640 *Web:* www.pello.com.au

A little slice of Italy close to the heart of Sydney is the best way to describe this cosy terrace-lined street in East Sydney. Brimming with eateries and drinking spots, cafes line both sides of the street with a few fine dining restaurants such as Beppi's (traditionally a celebrity favourite) and the traditional Lord Roberts Hotel slotted in between. Try Bill & Tony's for a cheap and cheerful bowl of pasta or one of the best cappuccinos in town. Bar Reggio is just around the corner (135 Crown Street) for delicious pizza, where plenty of PRs and local faces go for a good, cheap meal. If you're after something a bit more upmarket, try Pello—they serve up delicious morsels on their mezze tasting plate and gorgeous peach Bellinis.

Celeb Scoop: Naomi Watts loves the cheap and cheerful atmosphere of Bill & Tony's, as does Russell Crowe, whose autographed picture from *Cinderella Man* sits on the mantle piece. He often has coffee there with millionaire businessman Peter Holmes a Court, with who he co-owns the South Sydney football team.

Sushi on Stanley

85 Stanley Street, East Sydney
Phone: (02) 9357 6465

The city has an abundance of modest sushi spots, but this little eatery on Stanley Street is a real gem. The service is speedy, the food is authentic and fresh and with Spin Communications—one of the city's biggest public relations and media companies—located close by, there are always industry types popping in for a quick bite.

Celeb Scoop: Tom Waterhouse, of Sydney's famous horseracing lineage, has been spotted here, as have Silverchair drummer Ben Gillies and fashion designer Peter Morrissey.

Harrys

80 William Street, East Sydney

Phone: (02) 9361 4650

It might be tiny but this little takeaway cafe proves that the best things really do come in small packages. Banana bread, fruit, smoothies and great coffee or chai lattes can all be picked up to go.

Celeb Scoop: Actor Jessica Napier has been spotted ordering takeaway coffee here after an early morning yoga session at The Centre of Yoga (see index). Jess's caffeine fix is always with soy milk.

AAA-list

Tatler

169 Darlinghurst Road, Darlinghurst

Phone: (02) 9326 0222

Only those in the know are regulars at this Sydney nightspot, but those who are will agree it is a Sydney institution. The haunt that houses the 'too cool for school', this Darlinghurst den is popular among the social set, musicians, models and film stars. Wrought-iron gates hide Tatler's inconspicuous entrance on Darlinghurst Road not far from Kings Cross' infamous neon Coca-Cola sign. You must ring a doorbell to gain entrance (and entry is at management's discretion) and once the gates are opened for you, a stairway will lead you downstairs to reveal a funky setting which incorporates a touch of Grandma's house into its decor. Wednesday night is always a good night to pop in for a drink as musos like Alex Lloyd have been known to drop in and perform inpromptu sets.

De Nom @ Ruby Rabbit

231 Oxford Street, Darlinghurst

Phone: (02) 9326 0044

Situated on the third floor of Ruby Rabbit, De Nom is an exclusive membership bar in the vein of New York's Milk and Honey. The opulent room, with space for about 80 guests and the feel of a luxurious European palace, features gilded furniture, gorgeously attired bar staff and an aura of the rich and famous. The members' program is super VIP, with only 100 memberships offered at a cost of $10,000 each. Along with priority entrance, members receive their own private car and driver to transport them to and from De Nom on each visit, a concierge service, access to a members' only wine list, priority seating at events featuring international artists, a free event consultation service and use of the room for one private function a year without paying the $5500 hire.

Several well heeled local celebs have taken advantage of the solid gold membership card, encrusted with rubies and embossed with the De Nom logo.

Will & Toby's Taylor Square

Floors 1 & 2, 134 Oxford Street, Darlinghurst

Phone: (02) 9331 7073 *Web:* www.willandtobys.com.au

Four years of planning for brothers Will and Toby Osmond came to fruition in 2007 with the opening of this multi-million dollar nightspot. Floor 1 houses The Supper Club, floor 2 The Polo Lounge.

Celeb Scoop: When Jessica Alba attended the premiere afterparty for *Fantastic 4: Rise of the Silver Surfer* here in 2007, she was the centre of attention. While everyone tried to chat her up, Jessica kept asking them if they knew where she could get a slice of pavlova.

Galleries & museums

Brett Whiteley Studio

2 Raper Street, Surry Hills

Phone: (02) 9225 1740 *Web:* www.brettwhiteley.org

Artist Brett Whiteley's works sell for over $1 million today, and are highly sought after, their buyers relishing secrecy, to protect their purchases. Whiteley himself was a tortured soul, battling a heroin addiction, and eventually succumbing to it in 1992, alone in a hotel room. In the 1980s, Whiteley lived upstairs here at times, and had his studio, downstairs. Today it is an art museum dedicated to him.

Celeb Scoop: Bob Dylan was just one of many famous faces to head to Whiteley's Surry Hills studio when the artist was alive, to spend a few hours in his charismatic creative space.

Shopping

Vivid

558 Crown Street, Surry Hills

Phone: 8399 1210

Filled with babies' clothes, jewellery, cards, paintings, blankets, cushions and womenswear, you'll fall in love with lots of the stock housed in this delightful home and lifestyle store. It's a great place for gift-buying.

Celeb Scoop: Supermodel Linda Evangelista does get out of bed sometimes for less than $10,000, and browsed through the offerings of this beautiful store.

Wheels & Dollbaby

259 Crown Street, Surry Hills

Phone: (02) 9361 3286 *Web:* www.wheelsanddollbaby.com

Opened by designer Melanie Greensmith in 1987, Wheels & Dollbaby live up to their slogan of 'Outfitters to the Stars', counting celebrities like The Rolling Stones, Goldie Hawn, Daryl Hannah and Gwen Stefani among its fans. Think sexy posh punk meets Parisian scruff designs—it's all super cool.

Celeb Scoop: Fans of Wheels & Dollbaby's leopard trench coat include Deborah Harry and Sadie Frost, while burlesque star Dita Von Teese loves the Muskateer Shirts and Gangster Dresses. Pamela Anderson owns a 'F**k Off I'm With The Band' singlet and Hugh Heffner's one-time 'girlfriend' Bridget once wore the 'pink delicious cake dress' to the Playmate of the Year party.

Bakkatcha

Shop 33, 277 Crown Street, Surry Hills

Phone: (02) 9332 3583

Sydney loves a good frock store and this Crown Street store has so many to choose from. Take your cash or card and shop at your own risk—just be sure to clear room in your suitcase first.

'There are some great designers on Crown Street'.
Natalie Imbruglia, singer/songwriter

Style Brazil

277 Bourke Street, Redfern East

Phone: 0411 876 360 *Web:* www.stylebrazil.com.au

Heels so hot they'd feature on *Sex and the City* if it was still showing ... that's what you'll find here. Premium leather shoes direct from the warehouse that you won't find anywhere else, or on anyone else's feet. None of Sydney's style set share this top-secret shoe store with anybody—it's *that* good.

Also on The A-list
The House of Iona

2 Darley Street, Darlinghurst

In a grand, historic mansion is the office of Bazmark Inq, the production company of film-maker Baz Luhrmann and costume designer Catherine Martin, who just happens to be Luhrmann's wife. Many big-screen costume designs have been created here, including decadent, memorable designs for *Strictly Ballroom, Moulin Rouge* and *Romeo + Juliet.*

'One of the great things about Sydney is that it has a great acceptance of everyone and everything. It's an incredibly tolerant city with a huge multicultural basis. It's a city where you can be anyone you want to be. It's certainly got its own edge.'
Baz Luhrmann, film-maker

The Beauty Room

220 Goulburn Street, Darlinghurst

Phone: (02) 9212 4844 *Web:* www.thebeautyroom.com.au

So what if celebs favour Double Bay beauty and eyebrow guru Sharon-Lee? Who has weeks to wait for a pampering appointment? The undisputed eyebrow queen of the city runs The Beauty Room. Visit this tiny beauty oasis a few steps from the hustle and bustle of Oxford Street or head over the Harbour Bridge for a more luxe day spa experience at the Beauty Room, Mosman.

Celeb Scoop: *Home and Away*'s Ada Nicodemou and Isabel Lucas have been pampered here.

Brad Ngata Hair Direction

273-275 Goulburn Street, Darlinghurst

Phone: (02) 9281 1220 *Web:* www.bradngata.com.au

Brad Ngata is the darling hairdresser of the celebrity set, and his list of well known clients is a mile long. The salon is modern and upmarket, and the staff mantra is to treat everyone like a star. Brad is not always in-house, as he is in demand at fashion parades and hair shows but the staff know how to give everyone that celebrity look.

Celeb Scoop: Brad's clients include Portia de Rossi, Abbie Cornish, model Kirsty Hinz, Rachel Hunter, Jennifer Hawkins, Brian McFadden and Delta Goodrem.

RAW

95 Oxford Street, Darlinghurst

Phone: (02) 9380 5370

A recipient of the Hairdresser of the Year award, Anthony Nader is one of the city stylists constantly being bombarded by celebrity requests to tend to their tresses. A good stylist never reveals his celebrity clients' secrets but you might uncover some for yourself if you pop in for a blowdry at this beautiful multi-level salon.

The Centre of Yoga

Level 3, 85 William Street, East Sydney

Phone: (02) 9328 2085 *Web:* www.thecentreofyoga.com.au

Yoga is credited by many actors for maintaining their super svelte bodies and Janie Larmour's Zen Ki yoga focuses on body and mind, helping to rebalance your energies and improve your body.

City Gym

107–113 Crown Street, East Sydney

Phone: (02) 9360 6247 *Web:* www.citygym.com.au

Don't be put off by the muscle men who train at this fitness institution. Known by the fitness-obsessed as 'Muscle Gym', this was the first gym in Australia to ever run aerobics classes and there's any number of high-profile clientele who seek out the services of personal trainers including Olympic swimmers Geoff Huegill and Michael Engelsmann. Open 5 am to midnight on weeknights, and late on weekends, the gym underwent a major renovation in 2007 installing the latest weight and cardio equipment and adding a separate yoga and pilates studio and even free internet.

Bondi & City Beaches

'I feel blessed to live in a city like this. It has a great energy and vibe. I love the people, I love the beaches and the lifestyle. I love that my home is here.' Megan Gale, model

The city that is home to some of the country's most glamorous bodies has a long list of spectacular neighbouring beachside suburbs. Of all the beachside suburbs stretching from Sydney's eastern to southern coastlines, it's **Bondi** which is the mecca for all of the city's trendy glam set, not to mention local and visiting famous identities.

International star Cameron Diaz lived in Bondi when she was an unknown model, long before she found fame as an actress, and long before she met Justin Timberlake. Naomi Watts also owned an apartment overlooking the beach. Today, many aspiring actors and models choose Bondi as their home base in between castings and auditions. Head to this beachside locale on any given day and you'll see them: bronzed young 'frock star' wannabes, shopping on Gould Street and sauntering along Campbell Parade, strutting their stuff in oversized sunglasses and designer dresses.

Weekends you'll find them packed into Bondi's diverse array of cafes—Russell Crowe's fave is Fishmongers—overflowing onto the footpath, and hanging out in trendy waterside pubs, bars and restaurants like the Beach Road Hotel, Sean's Panorama, Bondi Social, Mocean and Ravesi's. On Sundays, you'll also find a posse of cool crowd types scouring the Bondi markets for bargains and indulging in peach Bellinis on the balcony at Icebergs Dining Room and Bar—a weekend regular for Heath Ledger and Michelle Williams when they were living in Oz. On the rare occasions that these fashionable folk wander more than a few streets from the golden stretch of sand, you'll also find them giving their credit cards a workout at the enormous Westfield shopping centre in **Bondi Junction**.

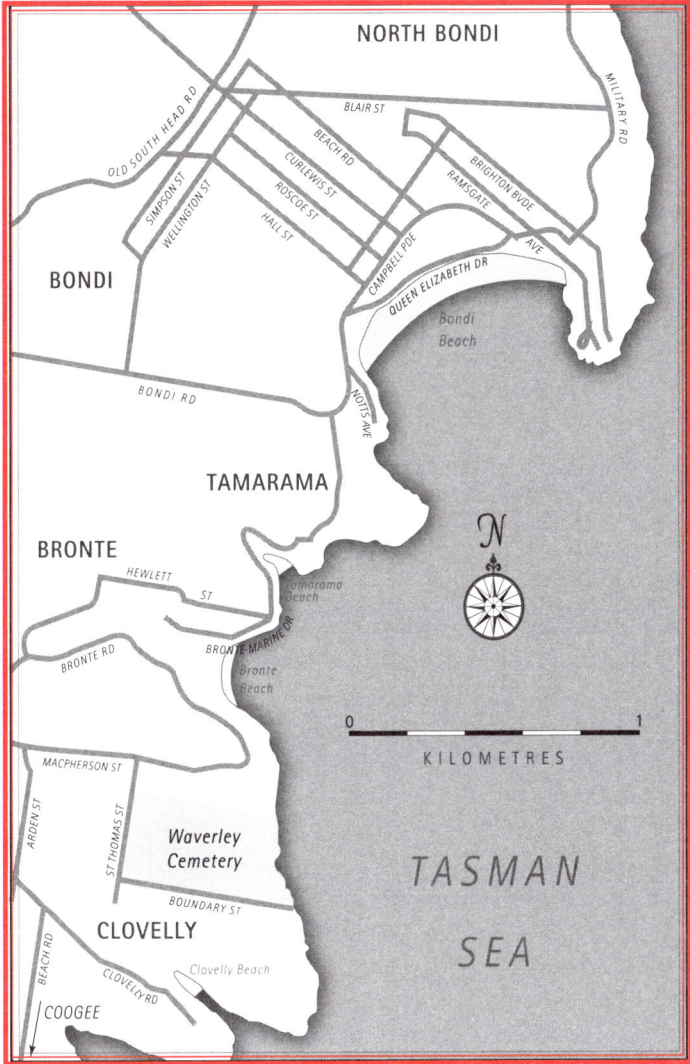

NORTH BONDI

MILITARY RD

OLD SOUTH HEAD RD

BLAIR ST

BEACH RD

CURLEWIS ST

ROSCOE ST

BRIGHTON BVDE

RAMSGATE AVE

SIMPSON ST

WELLINGTON ST

HALL ST

CAMPBELL PDE

QUEEN ELIZABETH DR

Bondi
Beach

BONDI

BONDI RD

NOTTS AVE

TAMARAMA

BRONTE

HEWLETT ST

Tamarama
Beach

N

BRONTE RD

BRONTE MARINE DR

Bronte
Beach

0   1

KILOMETRES

MACPHERSON ST

ARDEN ST

ST THOMAS ST

Waverley
Cemetery

BOUNDARY ST

TASMAN

SEA

BEACH RD

CLOVELLY

CLOVELLY RD

Clovelly Beach

COOGEE

Bondi and City Beaches

James Packer and Silverchair's frontman Daniel Johns both own apartments in the Bondi area. Other famous residents in the past have included Tara Moss, Wendy Matthews, Jason Donovan, Ben Lee, Claudia Karvan, Toni Collette and Jack Thompson.

Bondi's body-conscious beach dwellers make use of Australia's oldest swimming club, the Bondi Icebergs, and the magnificent Bondi-to-Bronte track, a 2.5 kilometre stretch which starts at the south end of Bondi Beach and finishes at the headlands of Bronte.

Australia's largest annual outdoor free to the public exhibition of contemporary sculpture, Sculpture by the Sea, is also staged along the coastal walk and exhibits over 100 works by artists from Australia and overseas. U2's Bono was one of the exhibition's 400 000 visitors in 2006.

Tucked between Bondi and Bronte beaches, is **Tamarama**. Home of supermodel Megan Gale, it is tagged 'Glamarama' by Sydneysiders in honour of the calibre of beautiful people it attracts.

Not far from Bondi is **Bronte**, a sleepy beachside suburb which becomes a hive of activity on weekends for gatherings and barbecues. Its cosmopolitan beachside cafes and restaurants are great for breakfast, lunch or dinner and are a fave haunt of local Aussie celebs including Christie Hayes of Home and Away fame.

Among the most famous to have once called Bronte home are Heath Ledger and Michelle Williams. Ledger bought a four-bedroom home on Hewlett Street in 2004 for $4.45 million (selling it in 2006 for $7.5 million). Film couple Baz Luhrmann and Catherine Martin also owned three apartments here—including a lavish penthouse—on Bronte Road, all of which were sold in 2005 for a total sum of $8 million.

Media mogul Lachlan Murdoch and his model wife Sarah have a $7.7 million home at Bronte, which they now use as their Australian base. (Prior to the Bronte pad, the Murdochs lived in a four-level harbourfront home at Point Piper. Despite its unbeatable Opera House vista, the $20.8 million property's stairs and lack of grass made it unsuitable to raise their two sons.)

Other spectacular beaches within driving distance—and very much worth a visit—include **Coogee**, home of two great sea baths: Wiley's Baths and the Women's Baths. **Clovelly** is also worth a visit for a snorkel or swim. Further south you will also discover **Maroubra**, hometown of Australia's best surfer, Koby Abberton, and former premier of New South Wales Bob Carr. It also features as the backdrop in Australian TV series *Love My Way*. Further down the coastal suburbs, a 30 to 40 minute drive from the city limits, you'll find **Cronulla**, local stomping ground of Lara Bingle, Daniel MacPherson, model sisters Tahyne and Cheyenne Tozzi, swimming star Ian Thorpe and world champion triathletes Chris McCormack and Craig Alexander.

'*I loved Bondi. I love Sydney. I feel like I'm a Sydneysider because I lived there for a long time. I took my kids everywhere in Australia ...it's just a very family orientated environment and that made it a lot less stressful for me, because people really did welcome my children with open arms.*' Lawrence Fishburne, actor

Hotels
Swiss-Grand Resort and Spa

Cnr Campbell Pde and Beach Road, Bondi
See index

Restaurants, bars & pubs
The Eastern Hotel

500 Oxford Street, Bondi Junction
Phone: (02) 9387 7828

The Eastern is spread over three levels and doubles as both a bar and a restaurant. Popular with the eastern suburbs set, a typical crowd here consists of Paris Hilton lookalikes and uber-trendy eastern-suburbs males with hair styled to look windswept and scruffy. Many VIP parties have been held here, including the afterparty for the premiere of Sandra Bullock's *Miss Congeniality 2*.

Celeb Scoop: Aussie fashion designer Peter Morrissey celebrated his birthday here in 2005. Another Aussie designer, Wayne Cooper, also doesn't mind a drink at the bar.

Icebergs Dining Room and Bar

1 Notts Ave, Bondi
See index

Ravesi's

118 Campbell Pde, Bondi
Phone: (02) 9365 4422 *Web:* www.ravesis.com.au
Directly opposite Australia's most exciting stretch of sand, Ravesi's epitomises the quintessential Bondi lifestyle. Fusing beachside accommodation, fine dining and glamorous nightlife, whether you're staying in one of the 16 stylish guest rooms—or the hotel's luxury penthouse—or having a drink at one of Ravesi's' two bars, you're guaranteed unspoilt views of Bondi Beach.

Celeb Scoop: Some big names turned out for the launch of pro-surfer Koby Abberton's MyBrothersKeeper clothing line launch in 2006, including the notorious Mark 'Chopper' Read, who Eric Bana portrayed in the film *Chopper*. This was also a favourite drinking spot of Naomi Watts during her time living in Bondi.

'*Bondi is great on a Saturday. There are so many people. Locals would probably go during the week, but if you're a tourist, it's great fun to go to Bondi. Great people-watching and a great atmosphere.*'
Natalie Imbruglia, singer/songwriter

La Trattoria ('Bondi Tratt')

34 Campbell Pde, Bondi

Phone: (02) 9365 4303

This local, unassuming-looking cafe is where celebs stop for a coffee, some brekkie or just to watch life go by. It has one of the best vistas of Bondi Beach, making it a favourite with international celebs.

Celeb Scoop: Look out for paparazzi—everyone from Salma Hayek to Hugh Jackman have been snapped at a table here.

Bondi Social

38 Campbell Pde, Bondi

Phone: (02) 9365 1788 *Web:* www.bondisocial.com

Described by a *Sydney Morning Herald* reviewer as 'seaside serenity, where calming wood and gentle lighting soothe the soul', Bondi Social is a swish, sophisticated restaurant and bar, with a chilled vibe and a drinks and food menu which are as impressive as the feature wall of wooden pieces, which fit together like some kind of oversized jigsaw.

Sean's Panorama

270 Campbell Pde, Bondi

Phone: (02) 9365 4924 *Web:* www.seanspanorama.com.au

Situated at the north end of Bondi, Sean's Panorama is a favourite among Sydney's celebrity set for its supremely tasty food. The menu is scribbled on chalkboards above the service counter and chef Sean Moran's clam and prawn chowder is one of the house specialties.

Celeb Scoop: Backyard landscaper, author and TV celebrity Jamie Durie is a regular patron of this Bondi institution.

North Bondi Italian Food

118–120 Ramsgate Ave, North Bondi

Phone: (02) 9300 4400 *Web:* www.idrb.com

This is the younger sister of Icebergs but it's just as cool, despite its laidback veneer. Perched at the other end of the beach, its corner position makes this a great people-watching spot. Sit back and enjoy a campari with ruby grapefruit juice while the frantic wait staff run round you in trainers, shorts and t-shirts designed by Tsubi's Dan Single, dishing out meals from a menu with over 50 choices.

Celeb Scoop: After dinner, head upstairs to the North Bondi RSL, where you might just find yourself chinking beer glasses with Missy Higgins, Nicole Kidman or Coldplay's Chris Martin, who cheered on Australia during the Australia vs Italy soccer World Cup match in 2006. Celebrity chef Curtis Stone is often here having dinner when in town and Cindy Crawford dined here with Gail Elliott when she was visiting Sydney in 2007 to open the Omega concept store.

Gusto

16 Hall Street, Bondi

Phone: (02) 9130 4565

If you find good, strong coffee and a laidback brekkie the perfect antidote to a big night out, then Gusto has just the right medicine for you.

Celeb Scoop: Filmmaker and TropFest founder John Polson always stops in when he is in Sydney.

'*Nothing beats early morning coffee at Gusto in Bondi, sitting on a milk crate, reading the paper and watching the world go by.*'
John Polson, actor and director, TropFest

Three Eggs

100 Brighton Boulevard, Bondi

Phone: (02) 9365 6262

Formerly called Brown Sugar, Three Eggs is a funky, unassuming cafe despite its bright blue exterior, and a refreshing mainstay of the sometimes pretentious world of Bondi hangouts. You won't find any attitude here, but you will find plenty of hearty menu fare. Head here for a big brekkie or brunch before tackling the markets on a weekend. You'll love the cosy vibe and its long wooden tables

Mocean

34A Campbell Pde, Bondi

Phone: (02) 9300 9888 *Web:* www.moceanbondi.com

The Tatler (see index) of Bondi, Mocean's underground location alone is enough to make it a hit with famous types. With prying eyes of passers-by on Campbell Parade unable to peer through windows, the live performances from emerging music acts guarantee that this place is always packed with stars—both established and on the way up.

Celeb Scoop: This well-kept Bondi secret is where music maestros Sneaky Sound System became the stars they are today.

'*I really enjoyed my time in Sydney. We had a great time there, Bondi was great. Australia is one of my favourite places; the weather, the scenery, the people.*'

Howie Dorough, singer, Backstreet Boys

Pavilion Beachfront

Maroubra Beach Promenade, Maroubra

Phone: (02) 8347 0055 *Web:* www.pavilionbeachfront.com.au

A refurbishment was all that was needed to smarten up the act of this old cafe. These days it's one of the fanciest eateries on offer in Maroubra. Sitting right on the beach that is home to Australia's infamous surf culture group the Bra Boys, the menu will surprise with its sophisticated take on beachside dining.

Celeb Scoop: Controversial world-circuit professional surfer Koby Abberton and his film-maker brother Sunny have been known to pop into the Pavilion here for eggs Benedict.

'I travel so much now and I love coming home to Maroubra and just having a good time. When the waves are good I love to go surfing here. I'll keep surfing all over the world until I die but I won't ever leave Maroubra for good. It's in my blood—I can't even live more than three streets from the beach.' **Koby Abberton, surfer**

Outdoor & adventure
Bondi Beach

This iconic beach is world-famous. Symbolic of the Australian lifestyle of sun, surf and sand, it's a magnet for international tourists and Sydney's 'beautiful' people. Trying to secure yourself some sand space—even on a one-kilometre stretch of white sand—can be difficult at times, particularly in the height of summer. The beach has featured in many local and international television series (like *Baywatch Down Under*) and feature films (in *Two Hands*, Bondi beach is the location where Heath Ledger's character accidentally loses $10,000 of gangster money while taking a dip).

Bondi was the subject of world media focus during the Sydney 2000 Olympic Games when it was the spectacular site for the Beach Volleyball competitions. Though the spectator grandstand erected especially for the Games was the subject of much controversy in the lead-up to the Games, the closest the venue came to any sensationalised activities came in the form of fashion designer Jodhi Meares (at the time Jodi Packer) launching her first line of Tigerlily swimwear during the gold-medal match. Ten models attended the match draped in white towels and wearing Tigerlily bikinis.

Media mogul James Packer can be seen regularly jogging on the beach early in the morning when he is engaged in one of his fitness routines, and the Flickerfest Film Festival is staged here each year at the Bondi Pavilion. Acting veteran Bryan Brown has also been spotted here surfing of a morning, while his wife, actor Rachel Ward, looks on.

Celeb Scoop: Billionaire Richard Branson once walked onto Bondi Beach and into the arms of several bikini-clad beach babes, who clearly impressed him as he remarked to the gathered media, 'G'day. I should do business in Australia more often!' Britney Spears caused a stir when she took a dip here in 2003 in her Ken Done polka-dot bikini, as did Paris Hilton in her white Louis Vuitton bikini, white shorts and signature oversized sunnies just before New Year's Eve in 2006/7. After a quick dip at North Bondi, Hilton washed herself under the public showers and then dried off with the towel of a chivalrous bystander.

'*I moved from the north side to the eastern suburbs. We had a beautiful apartment on Bondi Beach. Selling that place is one of the biggest regrets of my life. My favourite thing to do when I was living there was to do the walk from Bondi to Bronte. It's got a lot of rocks and cliffs and beautiful beaches. It's just a priceless experience.*' Naomi Watts, actor

Tamarama Beach

While Bondi may be Australia's world-famous beach, it's Tamarama that locals and those in the know flock to during the summer. Referred to as 'Glamarama', Tamarama is renowned as much for being one of Sydney's most beautiful stretches of sand as it is for the beautiful people who lie on it. Supermodel Megan Gale has a house here and can be seen regularly running the stretch from Bondi to Bronte.

Celeb Scoop: After swimming at North Bondi in December 2006, Paris Hilton took her distinct brand of party-girl glamour to Tamarama for a 15-minute tanning session alongside the beach's red and yellow flags.

Bronte Beach

Slightly larger than Tamarama, Bronte Beach is mostly frequented by locals—which is probably why it is often visited by celebrities including Cate Blanchett and Heath Ledger. There's a massive grass area which leads down onto the sand, dotted with barbecues and even featuring a toy train for the kids. The cafe strip is opposite the beach on Bronte Road, and is always overflowing with hungry beachgoers and sleepyheads on the weekend taking advantage of all-day breakfast menus. For seaside brekkies, Nicole Kidman loves the healthy options on order at Swell.

Celeb Scoop: *Little Britain* star David Walliams and Australian ironwoman Candice Falzon arrived at Bronte Beach and swam together to Bondi, stopping for a 15-minute kiss (serious treading water involved) 400 metres off Tamarama in February 2006.

'*Some of my closest friends live in Sydney. I stay with a friend in Bondi and that's my little hang. I like to get in my thongs, cruise down the beach and chill out, run, get a juice. The Bondi to Bronte walk is my favourite thing to do.*' Dannii Minogue, singer

Clovelly Beach

Follow the coast south from Bondi, pass by Bronte, and you will come to the narrow sandy inlet of Clovelly. One of the most sheltered beaches, it has an unusual Euro-esque cement area at the front section of the beach. Clovelly is a great place to sunbake and snorkel, particularly if you have children. Fabulous eating and beach snacks can be found at Seasalt, the cafe beneath the lifesaving club and overlooking the beach.

'*I just miss Sydney. I think about the beaches and the sea and the surf and how I'd love to be back there for summer.*' Dominic Purcell, actor

Shopping
Westfield Bondi Junction

500 Oxford Street, Bondi Junction

Phone: (02) 9300 1555 *Web*: www.westfield.com/bondijunction
Offering personal fashion styling as a shopper service and VIP valet,
this enormous shopping centre has been visited by countless high-
profile names, from supermodel Tyra Banks to *Bold and the Beautiful*
stalwart Ronn Moss. The centre includes a massive 11-cinema movie
complex, 22 places to dine (including seven restaurants and seven bars)
and the first of the country's Fitness First Platinum clubs. In addition to
late-night trading on Thursdays (open until 9 pm), the centre is open
until 7 pm on every other weeknight. Many designer stores and brands
can be found inside including Mimco and Zimmermann.

Celeb Scoop: At the centre's opening, actor Ronn Moss and
local hotelier Justin Hemmes got behind the make-up counter
and made over VIP guests. And just prior to the premiere of *Miss
Congeniality 2*, visiting star Sandra Bullock took to the red carpet
outside the centre. TV presenter Andrew Mercado got a little out-
of-control with his microphone, and Bullock told him—still smiling—
'Oh my God, you're putting it up my nose!' Kelly and Jack Osborne
also shopped up a storm at Westfield during their visit to Oz for
the MTV Australian Video Music Awards in 2005 and Victoria's
Secret model Tyra Banks shopped here in 2007.

Remo

98 Brighton Boulevard, Bondi

Web: www.remo.com.au
Owned by Remo Giuffre, this is the cellar-door operation of the mini
department store version of Remo which was in Paddington until the
late 1990s. T-shirts emblazoned with classic phrases and prints are the
signature items here and have a cult following, but there are is also an
eclectic array of collectibles from around the world.

Skipping Girl

124a Roscoe Street, Bondi

Web: www.skippinggirl.com

The cute, beachy look of this brand specialising in woven totes has attracted attention locally and internationally, with Barneys and Harvey Nichols now stocking the Skipping Girl range. For fashion that is fun and practical, check out the bags, clothing and accessories.

Luxe

110 Ramsgate Ave, Bondi

Phone: (02) 9300 8005

As its name would suggest, Luxe only stocks seriously cool labels with serious fashion cred. The decor is great—floor-to-ceiling mirrors and vintage wallpaper—and you'll find designs from Marnie Skillings, Sass & Bide, Tsubi, Gwendolynne, Mad Cortes and more.

Gertrude & Alice

40 Hall Street, Bondi

Phone: (02) 9130 5155

One of the funkiest second-hand bookshops around, Gertrude & Alice is also a great place to grab a bite to eat and have a coffee while you browse the endless expanse of literary finds. There's a second store on Oxford Street in Paddington but it's hard to beat the Bondi store .

Celeb Scoop: Hugo Weaving is regularly spotted here.

Puf 'n Stuf Retro Clothing

Shop 3, 96 Glenayr Ave, North Bondi

Phone: (02) 9130 8471

You might feel like you're visiting Grandma's house, but many celebrity stylists and costume designers have trawled through the vintage wares here and come up with a masterpiece.

Gould Street, Bondi

Forget tailored lines and conservative dressing: there's nothing conservative about the shops in this little laneway. Local retailers were disappointed Paris Hilton didn't call in during a visit to Sydney, but she arrived in Bondi to shop at 8.30 pm when all of the shops in Gould Street were closed.

• **Jatali** 87 Gould Street *Phone:* (02) 9365 2066.

Owner Tali Jatali is the eyes and ears of Bondi's—if not Sydney's—social scene and knows all the gossip, from where the celebs go shopping when they visit Sydney, to what the local TV stars should and shouldn't be wearing. Check out her newspaper clippings board to get up to date with local gossip in an instant.

Celeb Scoop: Model Megan Gale turns heads when she pops into the shop on a regular basis, and in 2007, Tali was distracted with an international phone call, and Megan had to get behind the counter and serve customers for half an hour.

• **One Teaspoon** 86 Gould Street *Phone:* (02) 9356 1290 *Web:* www.oneteaspoon.com.au

During a visit to Australia, Mischa Barton named One Teaspoon as one of her favourite labels. It's a highly sought-after Australian brand, often seen on local celebrities. .

• **Tsubi/Ksubi** 82 Gould Street *Phone:* (02) 9365 7044 *Web:* www.ksubi.com.au

Known locally as Tsubi and, since 2006, as Ksubi outside of Australia, this celeb-favoured cutting-edge designer jeans label has been around for quite a while. Initially launched and sold as Tsubi, a trademark infringement dispute in 2006 with US shoe label Tsubo saw the label become known as Ksubi abroad. The Tsubi/Ksubi signature style of stressed and ultra-cool denim designs are expensive but are a hit with both fashion trendsetters and celebrities. Bondi was Tsubi's first signature store; now they're all over the world. Sienna Miller is one of many celebs who loves the brand, and she has been seen wearing Tsubi's grey, washed-out skinny jeans. Kate Bosworth also picked up a pair of skinny jeans here while in town filming *Superman Returns*.

· **Grandma Takes a Trip** 79 Gould Street
Phone: (02) 9130 6262 *Web:* www.grandmatakesatrip.com
This spin-off store from the original in Crown Street, Surry Hills (see index) has the same eclectic feel, with the addition of funky children's wear and more beachwear and bathers.

· **Electric Monkeys** 80 Gould Street
Phone: (02) 9365 6955
Visiting musicians have been known to hang out in this spaced-out store, where vinyl from artists of all types, sounds and eras are on sale.

· **Alfie's Shop** 85 Gould Street
Phone: (02) 9300 6466
Guys who love labels like Tsubi, Evisu and G-star won't walk past Alfie's Shop—it's the only stockist for some of the UK's prime streetwear. And girls don't miss out either, with a range that includes Karen Walker and Lover.

· **Tuchuzy** 90 Gould Street
Phone: (02) 9365 5371
Word has it that Clare Danes, Lara Flynn Boyle, Kylie Minogue and Vin Diesel have all passed through Tuchuzy's doors. Hot labels here include Bettina Liano, Third Millenium, Sass & Bide, Gorman, Princess Highway and Louis Epstein. The boutique also stocks Santos Wish jewellery, a favourite of Bono, Rhianna, Beyonce Knowles, Jay Z, Natalie Basingthwaite and Sophie Monk.

Also on The A-list
Waverley Cemetery

Street Thomas Street, Bronte

Phone: (02) 9665 4938 *Web*: www.waverley.nsw.gov.au/cemetery
Waverley Cemetery has a priceless view out to sea thanks to its
spectacular cliffside location. The ornate and grand historic graves date
back to the earliest days of white Australia, and have made the cemetery
a great location for filming. Scenes from the Australian film *Looking for
Alibrandi* were shot here. The cemetery is also the final resting place of
writer and poet Henry Lawson.

*'It's a wonderful place ... green grass, blue sky, beaches. I really
miss it when I'm not here.'* Heath Ledger, actor

Star Residence:
Heath Ledger's house

99 Hewlett Street, Bronte

Heath Ledger bought his four-bedroom multilevel beachside pad in
2004 for $4.45 million with the intention of making it his base when
he wasn't working. He spent $2 million on renovations including
adding dark tinted glass to the floor-to-ceiling windows, and glass
balustrades on the balconies to counteract the lenses of hounding
paparazzi. Inside, Ledger chose dark timber and white walls, and a
huge collection of books lined the bookshelves. Following the birth of
his first child with partner Michelle Williams in 2005, Ledger hoped
to take some time out from the mayhem of movie-making. Ledger's
impressive home renovations did little to stop the paparazzi, however,
and an idiotic stunt by a photographer and a water pistol on the red
carpet at the premiere of *Brokeback Mountain* in 2006 left Ledger
and Williams shaken. The very next day, Ledger made the decision to
move his 'home' from Bronte to Brooklyn and Ledger's father listed
the home for sale for $7 million—at least a million of which was said to
be because of its star quality.

Kings Cross, Potts Point & Elizabeth Bay

'*Growing up in Potts Point was great fun. My parents ran Arthur's.... It was an amazing nightclub. I wish there was one like it now. I just remember crawling, literally, between people's legs because the bar would be so packed. Brett Whiteley and the Stray Cats I met there when I was a young kid.*' Claudia Karvan, actor

Undoubtedly Sydney's most colourful suburb, **Kings Cross** is also one of the city's most iconic. An epicentre of bohemian lifestyles since the early 1920s, it's earned itself a red-light reputation fuelled by its strong ties with sex, drugs and rock 'n' roll, and a long-running association with underworld dealings.

Along with the edginess such grittiness provides, also at the core of its identity is a neon-lit, 24/7 atmosphere and a blinking oversized Coca-Cola sign (which greets you on your way into the suburb), proof that the Cross has always been as bursting with glitz and glamour as it has been with crime and sleaze.

In the 1970s, Arthur's Nightclub was the place to be, especially if you were an artist or actor. Run and owned by the parents of Australian actor Claudia Karvan, this was one of the Cross' most happening clubs back in the day. Located in a old terrace house, the club had lots of different levels and everyone from Bryan Brown to the Stray Cats, Jimmy Barnes and Brett Whiteley went to Arthur's.

Thanks to a massive clean-up effort by the city's council, the Cross is slowly beginning to distance itself from its seedy stereotype and for every adult parlour and strip club lining its infamous strip, there's a funky cafe, bar, deli, restaurant or noteable place of interest.

New nightspots, cocktail lounges and fine-dining restaurants have melded into the Cross' lively and long-established environment. With

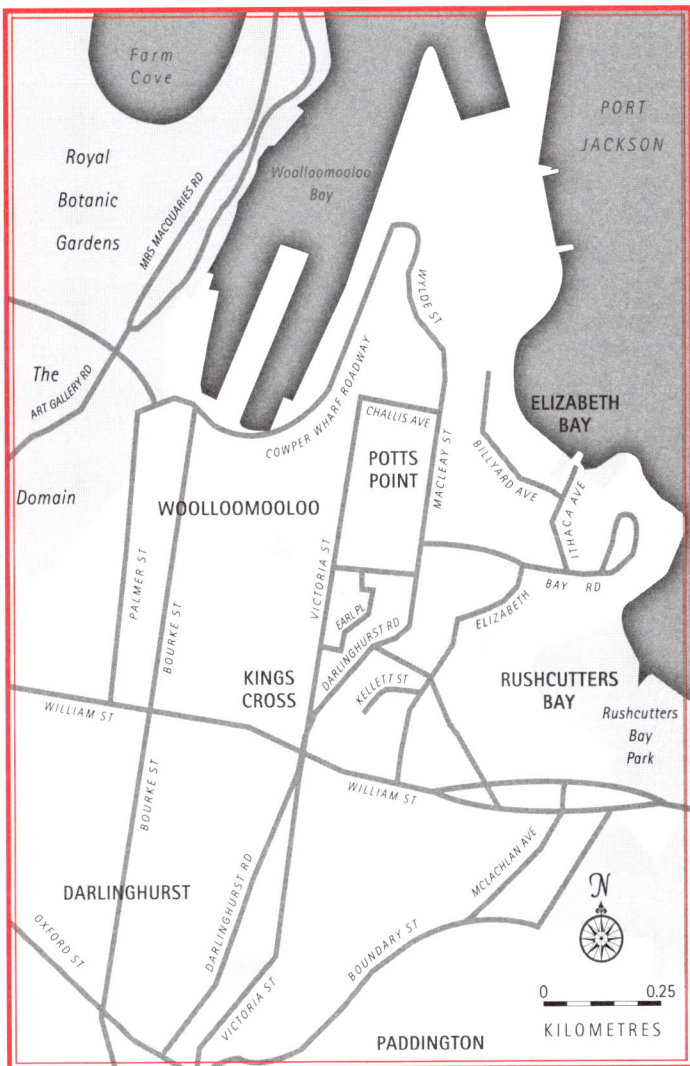

Kings Cross, Potts Point & Elizabeth Bay

the refurbishment and renovation of long-serving staples like the Bourbon and Beefsteak (now just called the Bourbon), Kings Cross has been given a welcome cosmopolitan feel and still managed to retain all of its old-world character.

The rich history and architecture of Kings Cross and nearby **Potts Point** and **Elizabeth Bay** residences have served the interests of many film-makers over the years. There's Boomerang in nearby Elizabeth Bay, a 1930s fantasy mansion that has been regularly used in movies (such as *Mission: Impossible II*) and for celebrity functions (Jennifer Lopez held a press conference there for *The Wedding Planner*). *Two Hands*, the film which gave Aussie actor Heath Ledger his first big break, had the majority of its location scenes filmed in and around Kings Cross—and in case you were wondering, the strip clubs used in the opening and closing scenes of the film were *Striporama* and *Love Machine*.

St Mark's Church on Darling Point Road is one of the area's most famous churches, thanks to its appearance in *Muriel's Wedding* (this is where Toni Collette's character Muriel marries at the end of the film). It was also where Elton John married on Valentine's Day in 1984.

In the Cross, you can get whatever you want, whenever you want it—both the Empire Hotel and Kings Cross Hotel have a 24-hour licence seven days a week. You're likely to bump into the who's who of the celebrity world every time you visit. Manage to slip by the doormen at Hugo's Lounge and you could find yourself rubbing shoulders with supermodels and stars, such as Heath Ledger, Heather Graham, Paris Hilton, Elle Macpherson and Megan Gale.

If you're in the heart of the Cross, be sure to look inside the many tattoo parlours on Darlinghurst Road, as there have been quite a few celebrities who have received permanent markings here, including members of Westlife and Australian boxer Anthony Mundine.

Just nearby, the Pomeroy apartment block is becoming the talk of the town for its celebrity resident list. Rumour has it that Dame Joan Sutherland and actor Naomi Watts both own apartments in the block.

Hotels
Regents Court Hotel

18 Springfield Avenue, Potts Point
See index

Medusa Hotel

267 Darlinghurst Road, Darlinghurst
See index

Devere Hotel

44-46 Macleay Street, Potts Point
See index

'*In the beginning I finished drama school and I worked at the Hyatt Kingsgate in the Cross (which is now Zenith Residences), and I was doing night shifts as a porter. I was 20 years old and fairly optimistic and self-assured, quite cocky, 'cause after I got a day's work on Police Rescue, I quit my job at the hotel.*' **Joel Edgerton, actor**

Restaurants, bars & pubs
Bayswater Brasserie

32 Bayswater Road, Kings Cross
Phone: (02) 9357 2177 *Web:* www.bayswaterbrasserie.com.au
Number four on *Bartender's* magazine's inaugural list of the world's top 20 bars, Bayswater Brasserie is a longstanding icon of the Sydney bar scene. The Bayswater attracts a more self-deprecating type of celeb who wants to avoid being recognised across the road at Hugo's.

Celeb Scoop: Kate Bosworth partied very hard here one night at the wrap party for *Superman Returns*, but paid for it with a shocking hangover the following day.

Hugo's Lounge and Hugo's Bar Pizza

33 Bayswater Road, Kings Cross

Phone: (02) 9357 4411 ***Web:*** www.hugos.com.au

The unofficial headquarters of Sydney's beautiful set, Hugo's Lounge is an exclusive clubhouse of cool with some of the toughest door police in town. Attracting a triple-A, triple-glam crowd every night it opens for business (Thursday to Sunday), Elle Macpherson, Michael Bublé, Paris Hilton, Heath Ledger and Heather Graham are just a tiny few of the many big names who have visited Hugo's Lounge. The neighbouring Hugo's Bar Pizza is just as popular. Duran Duran popped in for a gourmet pizza in 2004.

Celeb Scoop: Paris Hilton tried to party incognito at Hugo's Lounge one evening just before Christmas in 2006, attempting to mask her trademark blonde locks with a brunette wig. She needn't have bothered, though—there were so many Paris lookalikes in the house that night, star-spotters would have been hard-pressed getting the real Paris Hilton to stand up!

'*The best looking guys and girls drink at Hugo's Lounge in Kings Cross ... Mind you, it ain't that hard to find a beautiful woman in Sydney.*' **Nick Giannopoulos, Australian actor**

Le Panic

20 Bayswater Road, Kings Cross

Phone: (02) 9368 0763 ***Web***: www.lepanic.com.au

In the 1990s, Le Panic was called Sugareef. Since then it's had a thoroughly modern renovation. The owners are the same, and so are the crowd of beautiful people attracted to this happening nightspot.

'*Sydney's beautiful people hang out at Le Panic on a Friday night.*' **Sarah Murdoch, model**

Moulin Rouge Downunder

39 Darlinghurst Road, Kings Cross

Phone: (02) 8354 1711 *Web:* www.moulinrougesydney.com.au

If you're more of a party pooper than party person, you will need to set your alarm for this club, as the shenanigans here don't kick off until late. The hottest DJs are in residence and play weekly.

Celeb Scoop: You can order a Green Fairy cocktail here. Containing absinthe, it is named after Kylie Minogue and her role as the green fairy in the film *Moulin Rouge.*

The Bourbon

24 Darlinghurst Road, Kings Cross

Phone: (02) 9358 1144 *Web:* www.thebourbon.com.au

Known as The Bourbon and Beefsteak for many years, in the early 00s this Kings Cross institution received a much-needed makeover. Today, it remains a fave haunt of visiting sailors because of its close proximity to the naval base at Woolloomooloo. Upstairs is its nightclub, The Cross. Accessed by a separate entrance, The Cross only became so named in 2006 (formerly it was Plan B) where Darren Hayes of Savage Garden fame has been seen soaking up the atmosphere.

Celeb Scoop: This was one of the first venues to serve Ayala Zero Dosage champagne at the Chadwick's Model Management thirtieth birthday party in 2006. Produced by Bollinger, the champagne keeps the model set happy with its low-calorie content.

Goodies Milk Bar

58 Darlinghurst Road, Kings Cross

Phone: (02) 9368 0441

Even former political leaders like Gough Whitlam need a milk bar meal now and then. Goodies is a Kings Cross stalwart serving up all your favourite milk bar classics, like burgers, Pluto pups and hot chips.

Sapphire Suite

2 Kellett Street, Kings Cross
Phone: (02) 9331 0058

Over $1 million was spent transforming the smallish-sized Sapphire Suite into its present mod-funk state (formerly it was a seedy techno venue).

Celeb Scoop: During the height of Ian Thorpe's world record-breaking swimming career, the Thorpedo was spotted on more than one occasion inside this trendy lounge, and it's always a hit with the social set, soapie stars and publicists for media launches.

'*There's a bar called Soho in Kings Cross that I'd go to. And I had my eighteenth birthday there in a small club called The Freezer. In those days, I had aspirations to become a dancer, so I did a dance routine. I actually performed at my eighteenth birthday! I don't know what I was thinking.*' **Naomi Watts, actor**

Soho Bar and Lounge and Yu Nightclub

171 Victoria Street, Potts Point
Phone: (02) 9358 6511 *Web:* www.sohobar.com.au

From film stars (Tom Cruise) to British royalty (Prince Harry), sports identities (Candice Falzon) and pop princesses (Kylie Minogue), Soho has long been popular with cool media types, from the fashion set to hard rockers. Low-key and intimately lit, here you could easily be within a few metres of some celebrity heavyweights and not even realise it. Next door is Yu Nightclub, a start-of-the-art dance club.

Celeb Scoop: Soho is the place where pop princess Kylie Minogue reportedly met rock king Michael Hutchence in 1990—she started dating him soon after. Yu hosted men's mag *FHM*'s annual Girl Next Door competition here, where magazine types mingled with models and celebs.

Macleay Street, Potts Point

Macleay Street is where all the action is in Sydney's Potts Point. Home to a large array of scrumptiously stocked cafes, restaurants and bars, you'll often find many a celeb here trying to sneak in an inconspicuous Sunday brunch at Zinc, or an evening cocktail at Lotus Bar.

- **Macleay on Manning** Shop 1/85 Macleay Street
  Phone: (02) 9331 4100

  A beautiful homewares and gift shop. Everything from hand cream to artwork and stuffed dogs (truly) can be found here.

- **Macleay Street Bistro** 73a Macleay Street
  Phone: (02) 9358 4891

  The good, solid bistro food here keeps the crowds coming back. A favourite with film directors and actors.

- **Zinc** 77 Macleay Street
  Phone: (02) 9358 6777

  Consistent, fresh well priced fare for breakfast, lunch and dinner seven days makes this a great place for a stop at any time, as many well known faces already know.

Celeb Scoop: Not long after they began dating, in 2005, Delta Goodrem and her Irish beau Brian McFadden caused quite a stir when they cruised Macleay Street in a black convertible Porsche with the roof off. Australian actor David Wenham is a local resident.

Fratelli Paradiso

12-16 Challis Ave, Potts Point
Phone: (02) 9357 1744

Fratelli is simply a great place to eat. The food is fresh, the wine list is impressive and the decor is as slick as the clientele. You can't make bookings here (as with many of the best eateries in Sydney), but don't let that deter you as it is a hit with the celeb set including Jamie Durie and actor Leeana Walsman, who loves Fratelli's chocolate cake.

Lotus

22 Challis Ave, Potts Point

Phone: (02) 9326 9000 ***Web:*** www.merivale.com.au

Just what you'd expect from Sydney's hippest hotelier family, the Hemmes (who own the Establishment complex and The Ivy), cute cocktail bar Lotus is one of the city's seriously hip bars. Small and pokey, yet luxuriously plush, set foot inside Lotus and you'll feel like you've entered another world. Word has it that it attracts celebs who don't want to be seen, although the number of mirrors inside Lotus would make that a little tricky, since they're not only on the walls but on the tables too.

Yellow Bistro & Food Store

57 Macleay Street, Potts Point

Phone: (02) 9357 3400

As its name would suggest, Yellow Bistro is a brightly coloured venture combining a licensed bistro with a food store, located in one of the few remaining buildings associated with the bohemian period in Kings Cross and Potts Point from the 1920s to the 1970s. During the 1970s the building was associated with key figures in Australia's avant-garde art movement—film-makers, writers and artists including George Gittoes, Brett Whiteley and Martin Sharp.

Celeb Scoop: Yellow House was originally named after an idea Vincent Van Gogh had for an artists' colony in the south of France. These days the former arts-world mecca is more about inspiration of the culinary kind, with the desserts the big stars.

Dragonfly

1 Earl Place, Potts Point

Web: www.dragonflynightclub.com

This state-of-the-art nightclub is reminiscent of the type of dance clubs you find in London or Los Angeles, and the doormen are just as hardcore. Tucked away in an unassuming lane just metres from the red-light section of Kings Cross, and around the back of Kings Cross train station, Dragonfly is so good it is only open two nights a week (Fridays and Saturdays). Just as well, because its heady mix of partying, slate walls, seductive white marble bar, chandeliers, sexy lighting, young stilettoed crowd and shadowy nooks is rather intoxicating. Duran Duran, Jay Z, Beyonce, Usher, Black Eyed Peas, Ja Rule and Jamie Foxx have all hit the dance floor in this club to beat all clubs ... but don't even think about heading here before midnight.

Celeb Scoop: When party animal Jamie Foxx partied here, when he was down under to film *Stealth* in 2005, he liked to introduce himself to nightclub doormen, including those of Dragonfly, as the 'black Tom Cruise'.

'*I had a ball in Sydney. And yes, I did hang with Miss Australia!*'
Jamie Foxx, actor

Jimmy Liks

186–188 Victoria Street, Potts Point

Phone: (02) 8354 1400 *Web:* www.jimmyliks.com

Entering Jimmy Liks on a Friday or Saturday night will bring you face to face with Sydney's trendiest set. Think designer gear, plenty of flesh, and beautiful people. The cocktail menu is so good it rarely changes—try the sensational yet secretly potent Thai Tea. Split into two parts, Jimmy Liks features long communal dining tables on the restaurant side, and a sleek, long bar stretches out on the bar side. Best people-watching potential is from the banquette window seats at the front of the bar.

Iguana Bar

15 Kellett Street, Potts Point

Phone: (02) 9357 1940

One of King's Cross' old troupers, many rock stars have wandered down the back streets of the Cross to get to this understated bar housed in an unassuming terrace house. You can eat here until the early hours and then hit the dancefloor until sunrise.

Celeb Scoop: Many music legends have ordered an after-show beverage here, including Tom Jones and Jon Bon Jovi.

Gazebo Wine Bar

2 Elizabeth Bay Road, Elizabeth Bay

Phone: (02) 9357 5333 *Web:* www.gazebowinegarden.con.au

One of the only elite bars with an outdoor garden, Gazebo is the kind of place where you could easily allow your afternoon to blend into late night. The opulent bar is furnished inside with studded leather chairs and outside with French-inspired wrought iron tables and chairs. The wine list is internationally varied for wine buffs but is cleverly balanced for those who are better-equipped to bluff, with a menu that includes 'slurpables', 'unpronounceables' and 'pink bits'. Nominated for 2006 Australian Bar Awards Wine Bar of the Year, the *Sex and the City*-esque bar has also been an Australian Liquor Industry Awards (ALIA) Finalist for New Venue of the Year.

Celeb Scoop: The bar looked like the backstage of a fashion show when ex-cover models gathered to celebrate 400 issues of *Cosmopolitan* magazine. Guests included ex-covergirl Mimi Macpherson (little sister to Elle).

Candys Apartment

22 Bayswater Road, Potts Point

Phone: (02) 9380 5600 *Web*: www.candys.com.au

Its name might make you think it's some kind of adult massage parlour, but Candys is actually an underground nightclub (literally—the club is housed in two rooms of a converted basement). Established over three decades ago, Candys has always had a strong club and music following, and supports performances of new and established acts. Bohemian and laidback, check it out on any set theme night and you'll discover party-loving Sydney at its peak.

Also on The A-list

Boomerang

Cnr Billyard Ave and Ithaca Ave, Elizabeth Bay

This could be one of Australia's most well-known and film-featured trophy homes. Boomerang, a Spanish art deco home, was built in 1928 and was the most expensive house ever built during its era. Even today it is still considered one of the jewels of Sydney, and with its six bedrooms, 30-seat home cinema, conservatory, oak-panelled banquet room and deepwater jetty on the harbourfront, they don't come much more palacious. Its first owner was music publisher Michel Francois Albert, and the mansion is today worth more than $20 million. The house has had a substantial list of owners and breaks real estate sales records each time it is sold.

> Celeb Scoop: Jennifer Lopez's publicity launch for *The Wedding Planner* was held here in 2001. The high-security, strictly invitation-only press conference requested media arrivals two hours prior to its scheduled start time, and then began over one and a half hours late, with J.Lo making a spectacularly late arrival via speedboat to Boomerang's deepwater jetty.

'The weather here is great and I'm having a ball—riding over on the boat was pretty fun.' **Jennifer Lopez, singer**

Gingseng Bath House

The Crest Hotel, Level 1, 111 Darlinghurst Road, Kings Cross

Phone: (02) 9356 6680 *Web:* www.ginsengbathhouse.com.au

This is a traditional Japanese bath house, where you will be scrubbed and massaged like a piece of meat—but don't think about booking yourself in unless you're okay with baring all in front of strangers. Reasonably priced. Bookings essential.

> Celeb Scoop: This is a favourite pampering spot of Naomi Watts for a massage and a full-body scrub.

El Alamein Fountain

Fitzroy Gardens, Darlinghurst Road, Kings Cross

As renowned a landmark in Kings Cross as the massive neon Coca-Cola sign, the El Alamein Fountain is the area's only water feature and sits in Fitzroy Gardens, adjacent to the paved area where the Kings Cross markets are held on Saturdays. Built in 1961 to remember Australian efforts during World War II, the fountain is one of the nicer landmarks typically associated with Kings Cross and has featured in many movies.

Celeb Scoop: Look out for the fountain in Gregor Jordan's film *Two Hands*.

Sleevmasters Tattoo Studio

2/44 Darlinghurst Road, Kings Cross

Phone: (02) 8308 8074 *Web:* www.sleevmasterstattoo.com

Nominated as one of the finalists for outstanding beauty services in 2006 in the City of Sydney Business Awards, this is one of the Cross's best tattoo parlours, and the studio responsible for the body tattooing of boxer Anthony Mundine.

The Eastern Suburbs

'If I could take just three photos of Sydney they would be Elizabeth Bay House, Hyde Park at night and the lighthouse near Camp Cove Beach at Watsons Bay.' Sarah Murdoch, model

In a city founded on principles of aesthetics and lifestyle, the suburbs in Sydney's eastern suburban sprawl rank among some of the most desired addresses in Sydney—on one side there is the stunning sights of the harbour, and on the other, a picturesque coastline of cliff faces, beaches and bays.

Those that don't live here, aspire to, and those that do, are proud of the fact. Belonging to the eastern suburbs set sends out a message loud and clear that you are either one of the elite group of Sydneysiders wealthy enough to own a home here—like broadcaster John Laws, the Fairfax family, Nicole Kidman and Kerry Stokes—or at least have the intention of joining that exclusive club in the coming years. Everything here from coffees to car parks and even houses are at least 20 per cent more than anywhere else in Sydney.

A great way to see the sights of the east is to catch a ferry from Circular Quay to **Rose Bay**, a yacht-filled expanse of Sydney that is home to some of the best seaside restaurants in the world. Catalina Restaurant is as good as it gets, with sublime views stretching right over the water, sea planes talking off at all hours of the day, and fresh, superbly presented Australian food. Follow the coastline and you'll arrive at Watsons Bay. Don't let its fishermans' village feel fool you, property prices here are top end but thankfully, some of Doyles Seafood Restaurant's world famous fish and chips will only set you back around $10.

History buffs might want to visit Camp Cove, the location of the landing of the First Fleet in Sydney Harbour on 26 January 1788 (celebrated annually with a national public holiday) and also Macquarie Lighthouse, the country's first lighthouse built in 1818.

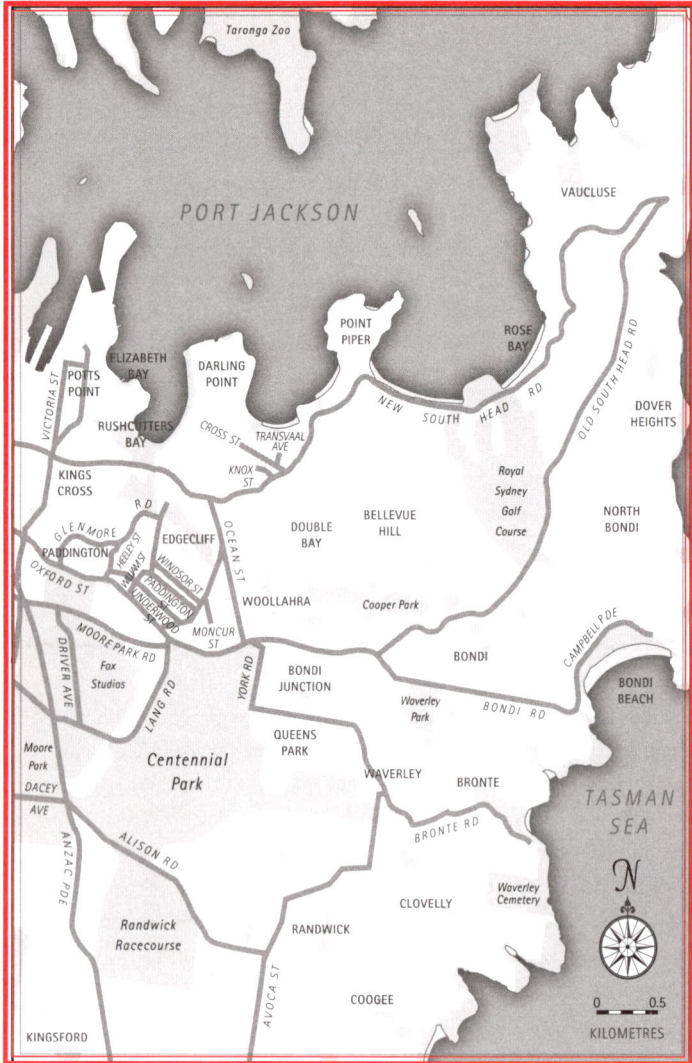

The Eastern Suburbs

For the most stunning views, wander up to The Gap lookout—just be careful not to venture too close to the edge. This spot has been the location of several high profile suicides and mystery disappearances—did they jump or were they pushed?

One of the east's most famous and popular landmarks is **Centennial Parklands**. A 220-hectare oasis (comprising ponds, trees, playing fields and lawns) in the inner city, the parklands stretch from Woollahra to Randwick. On any given day you'll find the park a hub of activity—horseriding, running, cycling, picnickers, rollerblading—basically anything you can do outdoors is done here. Marathon and road-cycling events were staged here during the Sydney 2000 Olympic Games and during summer, an outdoor cinema, Moonlight Cinema, is set up for al fresco movie viewing.

Just across from the Robertson Road entrance to Centennial Park is the Fox Studios Entertainment Quarter at **Moore Park**. Comprising retail shops, bars, restaurants and cinemas, what was formerly the old Sydney Showground, was transformed by Australian media tycoon Rupert Murdoch in 1997 and turned into a $71 million film studio/ entertainment complex.

The professional film production studios have been used for movies including *Star Wars* (episodes II and III), the *Matrix* trilogy, *Babe, Moulin Rouge, Mission: Impossible II, Superman Returns, Dark City, Holy Smoke, The Quiet American, The Night We Called it a Day* and *Stealth*. Stars from Britney Spears to Naomi Watts, Heath Ledger and Will Smith have all walked the red carpet at Greater Union cinemas here.

The New South Wales Golf Club, the Australian Golf Club and the Lakes Golf Club are a drawcard in the east, especially for sportspeople and Hollywood stars. During his press trip to promote *Rocky IV*, Sly played a round at the Lakes with his business partner and bodyguard.

Nearby **Randwick** is a hub for sportstars, soapie stars and TV hosts getting physical. Home to the Sydney City Roosters Rugby League team, the football players train at their home ground, the Sydney

Football Stadium. Fitness First's Randwick club is also popular with well known identities, including *Home and Away*'s Kate Ritchie who maintains her trim figure with spin classes and personal training sessions usually in the early morning. Vision Personal Training's private personal studio is one of the training grounds of choice for *The Biggest Loser*'s Australian series host A.J Rochester.

The country's finest racing thoroughbreds are trained at Royal Randwick Racecourse by some of the country's best horse trainers, including Gai Waterhouse. The racecourse is packed on race days with celebs and socialites and also features in *Mission: Impossible II* (Tom Cruise goes undercover here to swipe a memory card).

Heading north from Centennial Park and Moore Park toward the city limits is **Woollahra**. Filled with grand old houses and terraces, manicured gardens, designer boutiques and upmarket cafes, the suburb has the feel of an English village. Very much suited to its Aboriginal name translation of 'meeting ground', it's a quieter spot to spend an afternoon. Real Estate here is at a premium, with a basic terrace starting at $2 million, going right up to $6 million if it has a wide frontage and two car parks.

Lovers of historic homes will also take delight in the abundance of grand, heritage-listed buildings in the area, which are scattered among the multi-million dollar waterfront mansions in the east's most exclusive suburbs of **Point Piper** and **Darling Point**.

There's not a shop, gallery or even a cafe in sight in Point Piper, but in terms of celebrities, this is where they all want to be. Whether you are local or visiting, an address in Point Piper is the ultimate indicator of success. Houses sell for between $15 million and $30 million and come complete with super-smooth lifts, coffee machines, crystal chandeliers, boat ramps, multi-car garages, staff quarters, yoga rooms, cinemas and much more.

Temporary Point Piper residents have included U2's Bono, Naomi Watts and Cate Blanchett, who have all booked into residences overlooking the ocean. Kate Bosworth also stayed in a waterfront apartment here when she was in Sydney filming *Superman Returns*. Weekly rents start at around $4000 and include uninvited visits from determined Aussie paparazzi who pull up outside in boats with cameras and telephoto lenses.

Several years ago, **Double Bay** was the unofficial capital of the east, long regarded as the place to seen and be seen, full of designer boutiques and cool nightspots, but in recent years, it has steadily fallen down the ranks of Sydney's hot list. One stop remains a hot spot for celebs though: Sharon-Lee's beauty den which has a devoted following who only let the proprieter herself tend to their eyebrows.

Hotels

Sir Stamford Double Bay

33 Cross Street, Double Bay, see index

Kathryns on Queen

20 Queen Street, Woollahra, see index

Restaurants, bars & pubs

Doyles on the Beach

11 Marine Parade, Watsons Bay

Phone: (02) 9337 2007 *Web:* www.doyles.com.au

Synonymous with seafood and Sydney, this chain of seafood restaurants has been operating for over five generations. For indoor or outdoor dining, it's hard to go past the views at this seaside spot.

Catalina Rose Bay

1 Sunderland Ave, Lyne Park, Rose Bay, see index

The Pier

594 New South Head Road, Rose Bay, see index

Rose Bay Marina Kiosk

Rose Bay Marina, 594 New South Head Road, Rose Bay

Phone: (02) 9362 3555

For a more relaxed vibe, settle into the cushioned benches at The Kiosk. Perched on the end of the marina, it's the perfect spot to relax. No credit cards though so be sure to take your cash.

Centennial Parklands Restaurant

Grand Dr (corner Parkes Dr), Centennial Park

Phone: (02) 9360 3355 *Web:* www.landmarkcatering.com.au

Situated smack bang in the centre of Sydney's most beautiful parks, the Centennial Parklands Restaurant was used as the venue for *The Wedding Crashers* film premiere afterparty in 2005, when Aussie actress Isla Fischer returned home with her co-star Owen Wilson for the film's opening. The lavish party had a wedding reception theme— complete with a traditional tiered wedding cake. In true wedding style, many of the revellers got a little too caught up in the Sunday evening affair and were seen staggering, shoes in hand, trying to hail taxis at the end of the night.

Celeb Scoop: The raven-haired star of *The Wedding Crashers* revealed to more than one party guest in the bathroom how tipsy she was at the afterparty.

Arena Bar and Bistro

212 Bent Street, Fox Studios, Moore Park

Phone: (02) 9361 3833 *Web:* www.arenabistro.com.au

A funky bar in the Fox Entertainment Precinct, Arena is often called upon to organise the afterparty catering for red carpet film premieres.

Celeb Scoop: Will Smith and Nicole Kidman have been seen here as has Ryan Reynolds and Jessica Biel. Arena Bar hosted the afterparty for *Little Miss Sunshine*'s Sydney Premiere with Greg Kinnear and other Sydney film types in attendance.

Bills Woollahra

118 Queen Street, Woollahra

Phone: (02) 9328 7997 ***Web:*** www.bills.com.au

Another of Bill Granger's mouthwateringly good cafes, with a large outdoor courtyard. Try their hot chocolates, made with real Swiss chocolate, and their delicious brownies.

Bistro Moncur

116 Queen Street, Woollahra

See index

Zigolinis Restaurant/Cafe

107 Queen Street, Woollahra

Phone: (02) 9326 2337

From a long black to a three course meal in the back section, this is a popular cafe for politicians and well known faces. Great Italian style food.

Celeb Scoop: Tom Cruise has been seen dining here in the past, alongside many of Australia's politicians.

Pruniers

65 Ocean Street, Woollahra

Phone: (02) 9363 1974 ***Web:*** www.pruniers.com.au

Nestled in the green surrounds of Chiswick Park, Pruniers could be the east's answer to LA's The Ivy. Set in a lush, tranquil garden, breakfast or afternoon tea are popular. Dine here, particularly between noon and 2pm and you could just find yourself sitting next to someone famous.

Celeb Scoop: The who's who of Sydney's beauty world was at Pruniers restaurant for the glitzy launch of a new fragrance by Lolita Lempicka in September 2006.

Max Brenner

15 Knox Street, Double Bay
See index
Phone: (02) 9328 2555 *Web:* www.maxbrenner.com.au

Celeb Scoop: Australian racing royalty daughter Kate Waterhouse loves the milk chocolate frappes at this chocolate lover's paradise.

The Light Brigade

2a Oxford Street, Woollahra
Phone: (02) 9331 2930 *Web:* www.lightbrigade.com.au
This is a great place to rest during a full day of shopping. Clean, modern and spunky with a great restaurant on the first floor, it's always packed with good looking eastern suburbs types and often the odd celebrity too. This upmarket pub gets packed after race days at Royal Randwick and during sporting matches, with people bustling to watch events on a large projector screen on the ground level. Regarded by those that live in the east as a good place to meet girls and guys.

Celeb Scoop: Actor Kevin Spacey, Australia's answer to Jamie Oliver—Curtis Stone loves this pub, and Russell Crowe's wife Danielle Spencer has also been seen drinking here over the years.

The Golden Sheaf Hotel

429 New South Head Road, Double Bay
Phone: (02) 9327 5877 *Web:* www.goldensheaf.com.au
Fondly referred to as 'the Sheaf', this eastern suburbs set haunt offers four different bars, a great outdoor beer garden and regular live entertainment.

Celeb Scoop: Jessica Biel was often spotted at the Sheaf while she was in Oz filming *Stealth*.

Theatre, cinema & music
The Entertainment Quarter

122 Lang Road, Moore Park

Phone: (02) 8117 6700 ***Web:*** www.eqmoorepark.com.au

Many big film premieres have been staged at the Entertainment
Quarter of Fox Studios. The biggest for Greater Union Fox Studios,
and indeed the largest to have ever been staged in Sydney, was for
Britney Spears' debut film *Crossroads*. Fans waited from the early
hours of the morning to catch a glimpse of their pop idol. It was also
here for the premiere of *Brokeback Mountain* in 2006 where Heath
Ledger and his partner Michelle Williams were unceremoniously
squirted by a rogue photographer brandishing a water pistol. Deeply
upset and shaken by the incident, it is believed to have spurred
Heath's decision to sell his million dollar Bronte property and make
the US his home full-time.

> **Celeb Scoop:** It can't have been super sweet Mandy Moore's
> fault so it must have been the film company who only achieved a
> less than fair turnout to the premiere of *Saved!*. When Cirque Du
> Soleil's *Quidam* was touring in August 2004, Matt Damon went
> along to the circus show with his girlfriend who was accompanying
> him on the publicity tour for the *Bourne Supremacy*.

Outdoor & adventure
The Gap Lookout

Gap Road, Vaucluse

The sheer sandstone cliffs have a long running association with suicide,
but they do offer picture perfect photo moments—just be careful not to
stand too close to the edge—and a great vantage point during the Sydney
to Hobart Race, when the yachts berthed at Rushcutters Bay begin their
voyage south on Boxing Day (December 26).

The Lakes Golf Club

Corner King Street & Vernon Ave Eastlakes

Phone: (02) 9699 1311 *Web:* www.thelakesgolfclub.com.au

The Lakes is one of Australia's finest and most prestigious golf courses. Established in 1928, a round of golf here will cost you a rather hefty sum, as will a membership, which has a lengthy waiting list. Tournaments such as the Australian Open, Johnnie Walker Classic and Greg Norman Holden International have attracted golf's elite pros to this course.

Centennial Parklands

Entry via gates at Oxford Street, Paddington, Robertson Road, Centennial Park, Darley Road, Randwick, Clovelly Road, Queens Park.

Phone: (02) 9339 6699 *Web:* www.cp.nsw.gov.au

This is Sydney's largest public recreation ground (think London's Hyde Park). Celebs exercise here by the bucket load—but usually incognito. Popular with horse riders, cyclists and joggers, particularly on weekends, it extends over 385 hectares of grass, trees, and dams, and was the site of the birth of the Commonwealth of Australia in 1901. Rollerblades can be hired from Centennial Park Cycles, 50 Clovelly Road, and for horse riding, contact the Centennial Parkland Equestrian centre. In summer, the Moonlight Cinema provides outdoor entertainment, and polo is fast becoming a favourite for A-listers.

His Highness Shriji Arvind Sing Ji Mewar. At the annual Good Vibrations music festival in 2006, Snoop Dogg made a surprise appearance, performing his track 'Testify' in a Rabbitoh's jersey. He then left the festival and headed straight to Aussie Stadium to watch the pre-season clash between the Roosters and West Tigers. One-time lovers Orlando Bloom and Kate Bosworth used to walk Kate's dog in the park when they were based here for Kate to film *Superman Returns*.

'*I loved Centennial Parklands, I think it was modelled after Central Park. It's a big park right in the middle of the city and it's really, really lovely. I have a dog and she came with me to Australia so it was a nice place for me to walk her around. They hold a lot of concerts there as well. I saw Jack Johnson play there when I first came to Sydney.*' **Kate Bosworth, actor**

Royal Randwick Racecourse

Alison Road, Randwick

Phone: (02) 9663 8400 *Web:* www.ajc.org.au

Home to the Australian Jockey Club, horseracing events are held throughout the year at Royal Randwick though the racing social scene really comes into flower during spring and autumn. Sydney socialites and identities flock to the track to see and be seen in the hottest designer frocks of the season... and maybe catch a race or two with a glass of Moet in hand from the comfort of a plush marquee.

Celeb Scoop: During the Easter racing carnival in 2004, actors Jessica Biel and Jamie Foxx were 'sure things' trackside.

Southern Cross Seaplanes

Woollahra Sailing Club, 1 Vickery Ave, Rose Bay

Web: www.seaplanes.com.au

They're an odd concept—a flying boat—but they are the ultimate in luxurious travel. Southern Cross Seaplanes offers a variety of flights and packages—go ultra VIP and book a fly and dine option. After a 20-minute flight over some of Sydney's most famous and breathtaking spots like the northern beaches and the Hawkesbury River, the seaplane lands at the award-winning and extremely tranquil Cottage Point Inn Restaurant on the Cowan Waters. After a three course a la carte lunch you fly back home over Sydney landmarks like the Harbour Bridge and Opera House.

Celeb Scoop: This featured high on the 'must do' activity list for A-listers like former US Vice President Al Gore, Sir Cliff Richard, Cameron Diaz and Pierce Brosnan.

Shopping
Tim O'Connor

86 Queen Street, Woollahra

Phone: (02) 9328 9422 *Web:* www.timoconnor.com.au

Fashionistas with a penchant for print must visit local fashion designer Tim O'Connor's flagship store. O'Connor is the only designer with the rights to the flamboyant wallpaper prints of the late eccentric designer Florence Broadhurst. His garments are just as colourful, elegant and popular as Broadhurst's prints were in the 1960s.

Celeb Scoop: Tim O'Connor's store became a fave shopping spot of actress Michelle Williams during her time as a resident in Sydney. One of her purchases included a bright green 1960s inspired shift dress from the 2006 Spring/Summer collection.

Lisa Ho

2a-6a Queen Street, Woollahra

Phone (02) 9360 2345 *Web:* www.lisaho.com.au

Stars like Elle MacPherson, Olivia Newton-John and Jennifer Lopez are all devotees of Lisa Ho. Undoubtedly one of Australia's best known brands, Lisa Ho garments are inspired by the romanticism of vintage textiles and are beautifully soft and feminine. Purchase your own red carpet worthy dress from one of her flagship stores or David Jones.

Celeb Scoop: Delta Goodrem chose to wear a pink Liso Ho gown to the 2003 Australian Record Industry Awards—her first public appearance during her battle with Hodgkin's Disease.

Simon Johnson

55 Queen Street, Woollahra

Phone: (02) 9328 6888 *Web:* www.simonjohnson.com.au

Simon Johnson has evolved to become one of Australia's premium wholesale and retail operators with a focus on fine quality food. True foodies visit his heritage-listed Queen Street terrace store for luscious, hard to find ingredients—but they come with a price tag, a 750mL bottle of Italian extra virgin olive oil costs $52.75 and a 200g block of Valrhona chocolate is $20.35.

Celeb Scoop: Simon Johnson started out as a one man band, selling quality cheeses to notable chefs like Neil Perry.

Gary Castles

112 Queen Street, Woollahra and 45a Bay Street, Double Bay

See index

Empire

2/2 Guilfoyle Ave, Double Bay

Phone: (02) 9328 7556 *Web:* www.mrschow.com.au

Homewares and gifts can be found here along with Mrs Chow's cute range of custom-made wedding wear—Just Married bikinis and singlets.

Celeb Scoop: James Packer's wife Erica Baxter wore a white 'Just Married' bikini designed by Mrs Chow on the day after their elaborate French Riviera wedding.

Mother Baby Child

72 Queen Street, Woollahra

Phone: (02) 9328 3544 ***Web:*** www.motherbabychild.com.au

The ultimate designer children's wear and maternity clothing store, MBC is known for its sought after international collections. All of Sydney's A-list mums shop here.

Celeb Scoop: Citizens of Humanity maternity jeans, which were favoured by Kate Hudson through her pregnancy (they have an elasticised waist and cost $390) are available here.

Jones the Grocer

68 Moncur Street, Woollahra

Phone: (02) 9362 1222

The communal table at Jones the Grocer is a great place for a snack at any time of the day, just to read the papers (provided complimentary) and have a coffee, which Australian designer Collette Dinnigan does just about every weekend. It's a domestic chef's delight, with every conceivable ingredient for your pantry on offer. The confectionary is sublime, with chocolate, nut slices and marshmallows sold in slabs by weight. Or if cheese is your thing, this store is home to Australia's largest fromagerie. Try the Piano Hill Cheddar ($6.90 for 100g), a favourite with Australian food editor Donna Hay.

Celeb Scoop: When Kylie Minogue is in Sydney she visits Jones the Grocer to make up a hamper full of goodies.

Nerida Winter

10/20 Bay Street, Woollahra

Phone: (02) 9363 0822

Anyone who's anyone in the Australian racing fraternity goes to Nerida Winter for a new hat during racing season. Winter worked in the US, and then with designer Isabella Klompe in Woollahra before taking over the shop in 2003. Her raw materials and hand made detailing make her hats a must-have for any celebrities attending race events.

Bulb

10 Transvaal Ave, Double Bay

Phone: (02) 9329 5900

Bulb is designer Julie Lantry's answer to squashy stores with fluro lighting. She has created a sexy, boudoir-esque space with deep blush carpet, pink walls, rich velvet curtains and a vintage 1940s bar counter. Bulb loungewear and sleepwear is just as luxurious and extremely versatile, meaning it doesn't have to stay between the sheets. The basic slips and lounge pants are girlie and comfortable made from fine silk and cotton.

Celeb Scoop: Bulb fans include Cate Blanchett, Melanie Griffiths and Toni Collette.

Cosmopolitan Shoes

Shop 10, Cosmopolitan Centre, 2–22 Knox Street, Double Bay

Phone: (02) 9362 0510

Shoe fetishes can be satisfied in one hit at this high-end footwear store that stocks top-end designs including Sonia Rykiel, Dolce & Gabbana and Roberto Cavalli. This is the store Australian fashion editors visit to find the best shoes for their fashion shoots and you can be sure that just before any Australian awards night, the staff are working hard to fulfil orders for red carpet favourites.

Jan Logan

36 Cross Street, Double Bay

Phone: (02) 9363 2529 *Web:* www.janlogan.com.au

Jan Logan is the founder and chief designer of this Australian jewellery house that first opened in 1989. Logan uses the finest quality precious and semi-precious stones and South Sea Pearls in her crisp and original but always wearable pieces. Logan has been approached to collaborate with top Australian designers like Collette Dinnigan and Akira Isogawa for who she designed a special collection of jewellery to complement their collection for the Paris Fashion Week shows.

Celeb Scoop: Jan Logan's work has appeared on Paris catwalks in the shows of Australia's most celebrated designers, including Akira Isogawa and Collette Dinnigan. She produces pieces for characters in films and was responsible for the bling worn by Sam Neill's character in *Little Fish*. She has also designed for the acclaimed *Three Dollars* and *Ghost Ship*. Singer Jennifer Lopez was so enthralled by the Logan jewels she wore on loan in Sydney that she bought and wore them on the cover of British magazine *New Woman*. Logan jewels often decorate the decolletages of Kylie Minogue, Naomi Watts, Rose Byrne and Claudia Karvan. Nicole Kidman selected a pair of gold drop pearl Jan Logan earrings to wear for an Australian magazine cover in 2007.

CherriJam

16-18 Cross Street, Double Bay

Phone 9363 0555 *Web:* www.cherrijam.com.au

Revamped and renamed over the years, CherriJam remains one of the coolest night spots in the eastern suburbs. Everyone from the Pussycat Dolls to Italian crooner Patrizio Buanne have performed here.

Celeb Scoop: For the premiere of *Hide and Seek*, the entire venue was fitted out in keeping with the theme of the movie— complete with a Dakota Fanning look-a-like wandering the floor.

Camilla

6 Gap Road, Watsons Bay

Phone: (02) 9337 4444 *Web:* www.camilla.com.au

The Aussie fashion queen of the kaftan, Camilla's garments are adored by celebs locally and internationally.

Celeb Scoop: Stars snapped wearing Camilla's kaftans include Bette Midler, Sharon Stone, Tori Spelling, Jay Kay, Prince, Paula Abdul and Mischa Barton.

Also on The A-list

Fox Studios Australia

38 Driver Avenue, Moore Park

Phone: (02) 8117 6700 **Web:** www.foxstudiosautralia.com.au

Sydney has been the location for internationally financed movies set in Paris *(Moulin Rouge),* London (*Birthday Girl*), Mars (*Red Planet*), a futuristic city (the *Matrix* trilogy), a galaxy a long time ago and far, far away (*Star Wars*, episodes II and III), various international trouble spots (*Stealth*) and even Sydney (*Mission: Impossible II* and *Finding Nemo*). Some of these movies, including the two *Star Wars* episodes, have been shot largely inside the cavernous sound stages at Fox Studios. There are no tours conducted for the general public.

Celeb Scoop: Delta Goodrem filmed her film clip for 'Into The Blue'—the track she penned for her then beau, tennis star Mark Philippoussis—here. Renowned English fashion stylist Alan Keyes scoured local markets for vintage pieces for Delta's dancers.

'*There's something therapeutic about Sydney and being so far away—really, the other side of the world—from Los Angeles and the corporate mind-set of Hollywood. It's creatively liberating.*'
George Lucas, director, *Star Wars*

The Blonde Room

110a Queen Street, Woollahra

Phone: (02) 9328 6700 **Web:** www.theblonderoom.com.au

Step inside George Giavis's boutique hair salon and you will discover another world: a world of opulence and the ultimate in pampering, celebrity style. There are dedicated rooms not only for blondes here, but brunettes and redheads too. This stylist to the stars has worked his magic on many A-list stars, and even opens the salons after hours for his most VIP clients.

Joh Bailey Salon

7 Knox Street, Double Bay

Phone: (02) 9363 4111 *Web:* www.johbailey.com.au

Joh Bailey is an Australian hair stylist supremo who tends to the tresses of high-profile Australians and international visitors such as Olivia Newton-John, Judy Davis and the late Diana, Princess of Wales. His Double Bay salon was the first of his salons to open in 1985 and is a perfect place to retreat to for some beauty therapy.

Altona

Wunulla Road, Point Piper

Holding the record for Australia's most expensive house, having sold for $28.5 million million in 2002, Altona featured on the cover of the international publication *Private Sydney* as one of the city's best homes. Dubbed the 'ultimate McMansion' by location scouts, the who's who of the conspicuous consumption social set have partied here. The mansion has also been the setting for media parties society weddings and also doubles as a B&B for holidaying celebrities. U2's Bono allegedly paid $30,000 to stay here for one week and Naomi Watts and partner Liev Schreiber and Heath Ledger and Michelle Williams have also called Altona home.

Celeb Scoop: In August 2006 Mischa Barton made the most of her visit to Oz to spruik department store David Jones. She shot a TV commercial for local tabloid and gossip mag, *Famous* in just 30 minutes. Mischa was filmed barefoot wearing a yellow bikini covered by a sheer pink floral kaftan.

'*Queen Street has great antique stores and galleries. Great shops and cafes, too. There's a famous restaurant at Watsons Bay called Doyles. You should take people who've never been to Australia before. It's very touristy, but it's a great spot. Watsons Bay is just so picturesque.*' Naomi Watts, actor

The National Institute of Dramatic Art (NIDA)

215 Anzac Pde, Kensington

Phone: (02) 9697 7600 *Web:* www.nida.edu.au

Considered one of Australia's top two training institutions for actors, directors and anyone wanting a career in theatre. Entry is tough—on average one in every hundred gets through the lengthy auditioning process. Mel Gibson, Baz Luhrmann, Judy Davis, Cate Blanchett, Hugo Weaving, Richard Roxburgh and Tom Burlinson are among some of the successful graduates.

Celeb Scoop: When Sam Worthington auditioned for NIDA, it was only to support his then girlfriend who wanted to study there. Up until then, he was working as a bricklayer and had never heard of the prestigious acting academy. As fate turned out, Sam got in—his girlfriend didn't. They broke up and Sam went on to become one of Australia's top up-and-coming male actors.

'*I'd never even heard of NIDA, let alone knew what it was. I auditioned out of moral support for my girlfriend at the time. I just ran around and acted crazy. I got in and she didn't. They don't teach you the important things there though, like how to walk down the red carpet.*' **Sam Worthington, actor**

Paddington

*'I love it. I've already decided I'm definitely coming back, but
hopefully I'll be able to take a trip when I don't have so much work
to do and be able to enjoy the sights a little bit more.'*
Justin Timberlake, singer

Trendy with a capital T is the only way to describe Paddington. The
suburb is renowned for its boutique shopping, upmarket pubs and
art galleries galore, and it's also affiliated with a certain 'type': an ultra
cool, fashionable and affluent set of young, urban and ambitious elite.
Definitely not the kind of suburb where you venture out sans make-up,
designer jeans or attitude, Paddington is a playground for 20 and 30
somethings who have either made it, or aspire to.

To purchase a home here you have to be at the top of your field,
as prices start at around $1.3 million for a simple two bedroom
terrace (with no off-street parking), going up to $8 million for a more
substantial terrace home. Many successful, well-known Australians
have lived in these areas over the years including poet Banjo Paterson
(of 'Waltzing Matilda' fame), opera singer Dame Joan Sutherland, the
former prime minister of Australia Paul Keating, designer Collette
Dinnigan, and talk back radio king John Laws.

Famous in its own right, shopping strip **Oxford Street**, formerly
known as the Golden Mile, has always been top of the 'must-see' list
for fashion fans. Here you will find consumer labels such as Sportsgirl,
David Lawrence, Witchery and Esprit placed nicely alongside some of
the country's best designer brands. Charlie Brown, Bettina Liano, Sass
and Bide, Zimmermann and Alannah Hill are just a few of the big name
celebrity wardrobe favourites you can find on Oxford Street.

With Oxford Street's close proximity to the city's best hotels and
also the country's biggest film production studios, Fox Studios, you

might even make a shopping pal out of a local or visiting celebrity like Jessica Simpson, Kate Bosworth, Nicole Kidman, Mandy Moore or Cameron Diaz who've all paid homage to this most quintessential of shopping experiences.

The Oxford Street strip has come under threat in recent years thanks to the arrival of the Westfield shopping complex in nearby Bondi Junction. Thankfully, the preference real fashionistas have for street shopping and purchasing up-and-coming designs from the Paddington Markets (held every Saturday) as opposed to a mainstream trip to the mall has ensured its survival.

Another good place for boutique originals and hard to find brands is in the quiet and quaint **William Street**. A cluster of little-known designers sit side by side, making it the perfect place for interstaters to discover a new label and some savvy designs. This is where one major Hollywood star arrived expecting to be given garments and accessories for free but walked away empty-handed only to have her boyfriend return the next day to actually pay for some of the items she had her eye on.

More A-list visitors to William Street include Julia Roberts, Nicole Kidman, Ian Thorpe, Benjamin Bratt, Sam Neill, Mary-Kate and Ashley Olsen, Kylie Minogue and Tina Arena.

The real heart of Paddington lies at **Five Ways**. It is a junction of four streets, and captures the village feel of the suburb which enraptures the people who live there. Visiting celebrities love it for its village feel and glamour crowd.

Aside from shopping, Paddington has some of the best pubs in Sydney, and all are meeting holes for singles, sports fans, and the scores of young people who live and share the terrace houses which line every street. Prince Harry, Tom Cruise, Keanu Reeves and local actors are often spotted drinking in one of the area's collection of pubs (sometimes incognito), and whenever there are major Australian sporting events on, the pubs are packed with Australians celebrating.

A short cab ride away, the Sydney Football Stadium and Sydney Cricket Ground are home to regular sporting and concert events.

Performers from Robbie Williams to Prince, Madonna, U2, Billy Joel and Elton John, Barbra Streisand, Red Hot Chili Peppers, Bruce Springsteen, and Green Day have all staged live concerts there. A smattering of high profile names have also been there—to sit in the audience, including Michael Parkinson who usually spends summers in Australia, and loves the cricket.

Though perhaps not as popular as the shopping and nightlife, the art galleries are another staple side to the suburb. Many celebrities attend the galleries to survey the local art work and to pick up a new piece for their homes. Gallery owners are guardians of the celebrity visitor's identities, but on many nights in summer, the galleries play host to exhibitions, and high-profile names including Bill Clinton have been at the top of their guest lists.

Restaurants, bars & pubs

Boulangerie Patisserie Traituer

255 Glenmore Road, Paddington

Phone: (02) 9360 2462

Frenchman Frank Francois has been baking traditional French bread, croissants, cakes and pates from this tiny Paddington Bakery for over 24 years. His pastries are not only favourites with local celebrities, but he flies them out to events all over Australia, and even has a customer who orders his sausage rolls annually from Chicago.

The Royal Hotel

36 Glenmore Road, Paddington

Phone: (02) 9331 5055 **Web:** www.royalhotel.com.au

The clientele might be appear to be dressed casually in jeans, but if you look carefully, they're all designer brands. Numbers swell so much that in summer, the pavement outside is packed with revellers downing a beer on the Paddington pavement. The restaurant on the first floor serves good, solid, well-priced pub food but the real stars are the Elephant bar on level three and the top floor outdoor balcony area which has fantastic city views.

Celeb Scoop: Whether it was the name of this pub or the great bars that attracted her, the queen's granddaughter Zara Phillips enjoyed a few drinks here during a stint in Sydney.

Gusto's Cafe/Deli

2a Heeley Street, Paddington
Phone: (02) 9361 5640

This cafe deli has been in business for over 12 years, and serves classic home made Aussie salads, rolls, cakes, jams and chutneys.

Celeb Scoop: Soccer star Harry Kewell is one of many big names who have enjoyed a quiet coffee here.

Wasavie

8 Heeley Street, Paddington
Phone: (02) 9380 8838 *Web:* www.wasavie.com.au

A favourite with the Sydney media crowd, Wasavie serves up some of Sydney's best Japanese, from sushi to salads, cooked dishes and their specialty hot stone, where you grill your own meat on a hot stone at the long communal dining table. Like many of Sydney's trendier restaurants, you can't book, but you can leave your mobile number and pop across to The Royal for a drink or two while you wait.

The London Tavern

85 Underwood Street, Paddington
Phone: (02) 9331 3200

Unlike many of the pubs in Paddington, The London Tavern has yet to undergo a glam make-over, but it's cosy feel and basic bar food prove time and time again to be a drawcard for famous faces looking to go unnoticed.

The Grand National

161 Underwood Street, Paddington
Phone: (02) 9363 3096

One of Paddington's best places for food, often hosts Aussie celebs in groups of six or more. A tiny front bar with some great pub food, and a swish restaurant out the back with sensational wine list and food.

'Sydney has it all, the best beaches, great shopping, fantastic restaurants and wonderful people. The best pubs in Sydney are the Light Brigade and the Grand National.' **Jodhi Meares, designer**

Darcy's Restaurant

92 Hargrave Street, Paddington
Phone: (02) 9363 3706

Darcy's has been around for over 20 years, and the traditional Italian food is served up by gentlemanly Italian waiters. Nicole Kidman and Russell Crowe's wobbly autographs frame the remnants of a section of plasterboard, brought down during a big night at the restaurant.

The Visitors Book is more like an autograph collection. Shirley MacLaine, Mel Gibson, George Michael and Frank Sinatra have all eaten at Darcy's, and you'll often see the same autograph twice or even five times.

Lucio's Italian Restaurant

47 Windsor Street, Paddington

Phone: (02) 9380 5996

Another Sydney institution continually flooded with celebrities from Australian playwright David Williamson to politicians and media types.

Celeb Scoop: When working for News Limited, Rupert Murdoch's son Lachlan presented a black Porsche Boxter to one of his female editors during a lunch at Lucio's, due to her paper's high circulation figures. (It was parked just outside.)

Four in Hand Hotel

Cnr Sutherland and Windsor Sts, Paddington

Phone: (02) 9326 2254

One of Sydney's best (and smallest) pub restaurants with excellent beers on tap. You can't book for dinner unless you're a large group, but don't miss a meal here.

Celeb Scoop: Tom Cruise has been seen kicking back in this boutique-style Aussie pub.

Sloanes Cafe

312 Oxford Street, Paddington

Phone: (02) 9380 9818

The perfect place for a weekend breakfast and a home style lunch.

Celeb Scoop: The staff at Sloanes were left scratching their heads when Paris Hilton walked out without paying a $9.80 drinks tab, for a latte and a frappe.

'I love Australia. I had the best time, everyone was so warm and welcoming. It's great, I love it. I want to buy a house there. It's beautiful.' **Paris Hilton, socialite**

Mr Goodbar

11a Oxford Street, Paddington

Phone: (02) 9360 6759

A popular local night club with a mixed reputation that still attracts A-listers.

Celeb Scoop: UK chef Ainsley Harriott carved up the dance floor with some funky moves at popular night spot Mr Goodbar during a Sydney visit.

Jackie's

122 Oxford Street, Paddington

Phone: (02) 9380 9818

This unassuming modern little breakfast and coffee spot has always been a favourite with Sydney's A-list.

Celeb Scoop: Hugo Weaving is a regular.

Galleries & museums
Tim Olsen Gallery

76 Paddington Street, Paddington

Phone: (02) 9360 9854 **Web:** www.timolsengallery.com

The most likely gallery to celebrity-spot. Even some of the artists themselves have star status here. The Tim Olsen Gallery is one of Sydney's best. The gallery represents around 25 artists all of whom have either long established reputations or outstanding potential, including esteemed Australian painter John Olsen and David Bromley, a favourite artist of many local celebrities.

Celeb Scoop: Want the gallery that is a hit with Royals? You've found it: Crown Prince Frederik and Crown Princess Mary visited on their first return trip 'down under' from their home in Denmark.

Hogarth Galleries

7 Walker Lane, Paddington

Phone: (02) 9360 6839 *Web:* www.aboriginalartcentres.com

Bill Clinton had a stroll through this gallery during a visit to Sydney, and is apparently quite a fan of aboriginal art. Collecting it is a pastime for many rich and famous Australians, Americans and Europeans. Hogarth Galleries is Australia's oldest established Aboriginal fine art gallery, and is also one of the longest running private galleries in the nation.

Outdoor & adventure
Centennial Parklands

Entry via gates at Oxford Street, Paddington, Robertson Road, Centennial Park, Darley Road, Randwick, Clovelly Road, Queens Park. See index

'Centennial Park is great—it's right in the middle of the city and is the perfect place to run and hide.' **Michellie Jones, triathlete**

Shopping
Mambo

17 Oxford Street, Paddington

Phone: (02) 9331 8035

Founded by Dare Jennings in 1984, Mambo's bright, bold, eccentrically Australian designs have brought them to the attention of many high profile celebrities. The designs poke fun at art, politics, culture, history, music and every aspect of Australian culture they can think of.

Celeb Scoop: Actor Susan Sarandon shopped at Mambo for her son during a visit to Australia.

Napoleon Perdis Concept Store

74 Oxford Street, Paddington

Phone: (02) 9331 1702 *Web:* www.napoleonperdis.com

This was one of the first concept make-up stores opened by Australian make-up maestro Napoleon Perdis. Stores are now located in New Zealand, Canada and the US. Currently taking Hollywood by storm, Napoleon's fans include *Desperate Housewives* star Eva Longoria, singer Paula Abdul and actress Melissa George, who was signed as the face of Napoleon in 2007.

Celeb Scoop: When Sophie Monk is in town she always gets Napoleon make-up artist Anna Papadopoulos to do her make-up at Napoleon.

'If I could take the class of Sydney to LA, I would be very happy.'
Melissa George, actor

Alannah Hill

118–120 Oxford Street, Paddington

Phone: (02) 9380 9147 *Web:* www.alannahhill.com.au

Ashlee Simpson and Aussie singer Delta Goodrem love the eclectic style of Alannah Hill. The collection oozes femininity, and floral prints, a range of colours and a bright, strong energy are reflected in all of her collections.

Celeb Scoop: On a visit to Sydney for the Australian MTV Video Music Awards in 2006, Jessica Simpson bought two pairs of boots from Alannah Hill. The boots laced at the sides and were priced at over $400 each!

Scanlan and Theodore

122 Oxford Street, Paddington

Phone: (02) 9380 9388 *Web:* www.scanlantheodore.com.au

Talk about a star style guru. Gary Theodore's vision of the ideal woman (intelligent, passionate and independent) obviously strikes a chord with the most famous of the world's female celebrities. Pieces lean on the more reasonable side of exy, but they're classic designs that you will be able to wear even as seasons come and go.

Celeb Scoop: Kate Bosworth is a fan of this boutique as is Nicole Kidman, Cate Blanchett, Princess Mary, Micha Barton, Uma Thurman, Naomi Watts, Kylie Minogue and Mary-Kate and Ashley Olsen.

Sass & Bide

132 Oxford Street, Paddington

Phone: (02) 9360 3900 *Web:* www.sassandbide.com

With beautiful changing rooms and an equestrian theme, the Sass & Bide store itself is a spectacle. A popular brand amongst a huge number of celebs, Sass & Bide was launched in Australia in 2001, and is as well known abroad as it is here. Founded by Sarah-Jane Clarke (nickname 'sass') and Heidi Middleton (nickname 'bide') the label began life as a stall on London's Portobello Road, then rose to fashion heights with their now famous denim designs. Their motto is, 'Don't look too pretty'.

Celeb Scoop: Kate Bosworth has said Sass and Bide is one of her favourite places to shop in Sydney, and bought more than one pair of skinny jeans while she was in town filming *Superman Returns*. The brand has also 'guest starred' on *Sex and the City*.

Charlie Brown

178 Oxford Street, Paddington

Phone: (02) 9360 9001 *Web:* www.charliebrown.com.au

The effervescent designer Charlie Brown has featured international talent in her parades and advertising campaigns, including supermodels Linda Evangelista, Helena Christensen, Sophie Dahl, Jodie Kidd and Jade Jagger. Celebrities love the bold fashion on offer here.

Dinosaur Designs

339 Oxford Street, Paddington

Phone: (02) 9361 3776 *Web:* www.dinosaurdesigns.com.au

Dinosaur Designs is a funky homeware and jewellery design store with lots of multi-coloured frosted resin, plus some glass and ceramics. In 2007, they introduced silver into their jewellery range. Dinosaur designs offer original design contemporary jewellery and homewares.

Camilla Franks

258 Oxford Street, Paddington

Phone: (02) 9368 7666 *Web:* www.camilla.com.au

Camilla travels the world to source the most exquisite, and rare materials including cashmeres, angoras and silks for her designs. She creates and designs many of her own fabrics, which are detailed with exquisite hand-beading and embroidery. The label began from behind the scenes, back stage creating costumes for her Shakespearean characters.

Celeb Scoop: Elle McPherson, Sharon Stone, Prince, Kim Cattrell, Nicole Kidman, Jamiraqoui, Cate Blanchette and Bette Middler are just a few of Camilla Franks celebrity clients.

M.A.C.

276 Oxford Street, Paddington

Phone: (02) 9381 1200 *Web:* www.maccosmetics.com.au

A favourite with celebrities worldwide, don't be surprised to see big names shopping here for beauty items they may have left at home.

Jurlique Concept Store

352a Oxford Street, Paddington

Phone: (02) 9368 7373

This natural beauty product store hit the headlines in 2006, when media mogul Kerry packer bought into the business. It all started in South Australia, and now Jurlique brings naturally grown Aussie products to the world. A favourite of many visiting celebs.

Zimmermann

387 Oxford Street, Paddington

Phone: (02) 9357 4700 *Web:* www.zimmerman.com.au

Nicky and Simone Zimmermann are the design duo behind one of Australia's most popular designer labels. The brand is ultra sexy yet extremely wearable and their swimwear would rival even the hottest of designs you would see on the beach in Street Tropez.

Celeb Scoop: In 2003, Zimmermann designed a black ARIAs dress especially for singer Amiel to wear to the music awards ceremony. Australian radio and TV personality Lizzy Lovette is also a huge fan.

Mimco

436 Oxford Street, Paddington

Phone: (02) 9357 6884 *Web:* www.mimco.com.au

Linda Evangalista isn't the only star who has discovered this fabulous Aussie brand. Mimco is Australia's leading accessories brand, housing an extensive range of sparkly hair clips, jewellery, belts and bags.

Bettina Liano

440 Oxford Street, Paddington

Phone: (02) 9380 5771 *Web:* www.bettinaliano.com.au

Bettina Liano is a leader in the Australian fashion industry and her self-titled clothing label is one of our most highly regarded retailers and exporters. Liano is internationally renowned for her fashionably sexy, original Australian range of hipster 'O' jeans.

Gary Castles

328 Oxford Street, Paddington

Phone: (02) 9361 4560 *Web:* www.garycastlessydney.com

It is Gary Castles' Australian feminine, sexy, girly, heeled shoes which has kept him in the fashion industry for over 30 years. Castles was also responsible for introducing Charles Jourdan, Christian Dior, Walter Steiger, Bruno Magli, Casadei, Sergio Rossi, Yves Street Laurent, Maud

Frizon, Michelle Perry and Rene Caovilla into the Aussie market place.

Celeb Scoop: Kylie and Dannii Minogue, Toni Collette and actress Sarah Michelle Geller are well-heeled thanks to Mr Castles.

Fleur Wood

464 Oxford Street, Paddington

Phone: (02) 9380 9511 **Web:** www.fleurwood.com

This feminine designer, whose garments are stocked in LA and the UK as well as on Oxford Street is a must-stop for something special.

Celeb Scoop: While accompanying her then boyfriend Justin Timberlake to Sydney for his concert tour in 2004, Cameron Diaz headed here for a spot of shopping.

The Paddington Markets

Uniting Church, 395 Oxford Street, Paddington

Phone: (02) 9331 2923

Held every Saturday from 10am-4pm, the markets were established over 20 years ago on the church grounds, and provided a start for many Australian designers including Lisa Ho, Collette Dinnigan and the Zimmermann sisters. The markets are a Sydney institution and showcase mainly new goods including clothes, homewares and beauty products rather than vintage items.

Celeb Scoop: Plenty of celebrities drop in for a look, including Russell Crowe's wife Danielle Spencer, who has been seen buying jewellery here.

Victoria Spring

5 William Street, Paddington

Phone: (02) 9331 7862 **Web:** www.victoriaspringdesigns.com

In between designing dinner sets for Elton John and jewellery for movies including *Moulin Rouge, Mission Impossible* and *Muriel's Wedding*, Victoria Spring is designing jewellery for the stars.

Renya Xydis Concept

10 William Street, Paddington

Phone: (02) 9357 6228

Nicole Kidman, Toni Collette, Cate Blanchett, Naomi Watts, Geoffrey Rush, and Hugh Jackman are just some of Renya's clients. Known for her work in the top glossy magazines, this is serious star territory—but don't the stylists know it! Her other salon, Valonz, is close by at 20-22 Elizabeth Street.

Celeb Scoop: Toni Collette is a fan of the jewellery range that Renya stocks in her store, wearing one of the 'Hugs and Kisses' pendants to the 2007 Golden Globes. Renya Xydis was just one of the stylists who helped create Nicole Kidman's hair for her 2006 wedding to Keith Urban. Kidman also flew in her personal stylist from LA for her big day.

'I love living here, I make the most sense here. I have tried living other places and it doesn't work. So it's best to travel and work and go 'Woo hoo, I'm on the other side of the world' and then when I come home, I appreciate home being what it is and feel settled.' **Toni Collette, actor/singer**

Susie Mooratoff

11 William Street, Paddington

Phone: (02) 9356 2111

Susie has been dressing Aussie celebs for over 15 years. This unique little store is the perfect stop for party frock, wedding dress or even casual wear.

Celeb Scoop: Local names who have shopped here include Tina Arena, Kylie Minogue and Marcia Hines.

Sylvia Chan

20 William Street, Paddington

Phone: (02) 9380 5981

Celebs love this store—from Julia Roberts to Aussie singer Marcia Hines and more one-off Asian inspired Chong Sums, and contemporary, unique pieces attract them all.

Collette Dinnigan

33 William Street, Paddington

Phone: (02) 9360 6691 *Web:* www.collettedinnigan.com.au

Dinnigan started her career working in fashion for the costume department of the ABC in Sydney, and launched her own label in 1990. Now her garments are sold in Europe and America. This store is like a little piece of Paris sitting in the heart of Paddington, and even the store interiors reflect Dinnigan's attention to detail and classic, elegant, classy style.

Celeb Scoop: Nicole Kidman, Sandra Bullock, Cate Blanchett, Jerry Hall, Cameron Diaz and Kylie Minogue are just some of the many stars who wear Collette Dinnigan's beautiful feminine garments.

Tigerlily

37 William Street, Paddington

Phone: (02) 8354 1832 *Web:* www.tigerlilyswimwear.com.au

This was the first stand-alone Tigerlily store. The label was launched at the Sydney 2000 Olympic Games and instantly became one of Australia's hottest swimwear and lifestyle labels. Created by Aussie model, media identity and former wife of Aussie media mogul James Packer, Jodhi Meares. There's even a spray-tanning booth in the back of the store, so you can get a tan the safe way before hitting the beach.

Belinda

39 William Street, Paddington

Phone: (02) 9380 8728 *Web:* www.belinda.com.au

A popular spot for visiting celebrities, this gorgeous little store has produced many sister stores all over Sydney, although the original one is always worth a visit. Beautiful garments from a range of designers are presented in an intimate setting. No-one famous visits William Street without shopping here.

Celeb Scoop: A fave of Naomi Watts.

The Corner Shop

43 William Street, Paddington

Phone: (02) 9380 9828

This is a cutting-edge, boutique style store which always attracts visiting celebrities looking for that special piece.

Celeb Scoop: Aussie model Gemma Ward is a fan, who shops here for hand-picked vintage and customised pieces, as well as a range of designer labels such as Alice McCall, Sass & Bide, Anna and Boy and Josh Goot.

Leona Edmiston

88 William Street, Paddington

Phone: (02) 9331 7033

This beautiful clothing store always has something feminine on offer. Leona herself is often in the store Monday to Friday, but usually escapes to her Southern Highlands country property on weekends.

Celeb Scoop: Helena Christensen, Rachael Hunter, Kristen Davis, Olivia Newton-John, and Elle Macpherson are among the A-listers who have been photographed in Edmiston's garments.

Tsubi/Ksubi

16 Glenmore Road, Paddington
See index

Nicola Finetti Parlour X

213 Glenmore Road, Paddington

Phone: (02) 9331 0999 *Web:* www.nicolafinetti.com

Naomi Watts and Cate Blanchett are fans of Nicola Finetti's feminine, sensual, modern and individual garments. Born in Italy, the influence of Finetti's European heritage is reflected in his fashion which exudes a worldly feel that appeals to women from all global destinations.

Also on The A-list

Fiveways Cellars

4 Heeley Street, Paddington

Phone: (02) 9360 4242

Celebrities and the well-heeled media set are regular clients of this tiny bottle shop. It has stocked some of Australia's best for the past 20 years, and is a great place to spend some time educating yourself about trends in Aussie wines. If you're hankering for an overseas drop, there are Italian, Spanish and German wines.

Venustus

381 Oxford Street, Paddington

Phone: (02) 9361 4014 *Web:* www.venustus.com.au

Nestled among the hubbub of Sydney's bustling Oxford Street, a beauty and spa oasis awaits. Frequented by high profile stars, at Venustus Beauty and Body Lab everyone gets the VIP treatment thanks to their range of divine pampering treatments.

Celeb Scoop: Word has it that on the rare occasion when Nicole Kidman gets a spray tan, this is where she gets it done.

Max The Hairdresser

8 William Street, Paddington

This may look like an old-fashioned down market barber, but Max has cut the hair of almost every male actor who has visited Sydney. Located so close to Fox Studios, he is often called on set to create a certain look for a star, or to transform an entire cast.

Celeb Scoop: Tom Cruise, Hugh Jackman, Heath Ledger and hundreds more have all been subjected to Max's scissor treatment.

Tatjana Vaune Hair and Beauty

34 William Street, Paddington

Phone: (02) 9380 8183

Specialising in blondes and healthier organic colour alternatives, Tatjana is often on the road—in Prague or Russia working on film sets with Roman Polanski and other world famous directors. If a true movie star look is what you are after—go no further.

The Paddington Beauty Room

217 Glenmore Road, Paddington

Phone: (02) 9356 8700

The Paddington Beauty Room is where the wealthiest people in Sydney like to be pampered in style. There are reputedly only 350 or so black American express cards in Australia—and the proprieter claims 30 black Amex card holders visit the salon regularly. Great for luxurious La Prairie facials.

Celeb Scoop: Rupert Murdoch's daughter-in-law Sarah Murdoch is a regular—she always has a La Prairie facial. Aussie actors are also regular clients.

Christina Fitzgerald

Level 1/ 354 South Dowling Street Paddington

Phone: (02) 9368 0971

Christina was the original manicurist and nail expert at the Sebel Hotel, an institution in Kings Cross in the 1980s, as every celebrity who came to Sydney stayed there. With over 20 years experience, she knows how to give nails that star quality.

Celeb Scoop: There's not many celeb hands Christine Fitzgerald hasn't held from Billy Idol to Kylie, Janet Jackson, Carolyn Murphy, Lauren Hutton, Helena Christensen and Barbra Streisand.

Susan Avery Flowers & Event Styling

59 Jersey Road, Woollahra

Phone: (02) 9363 1168

The city's unofficial florist to the stars, Susan Avery has been responsible for decorating the home of Nicole Kidman when she was still married to Tom Cruise each Christmas. Similarly, Susan decorated the home of Elle MacPherson one Christmas, using Elle's favourite flowers—wild bush roses—inside glass balls which hung on the Christmas tree. She was also responsible for the flowers on set during the filming of *Moulin Rouge* and decorating the houses of George Lucas while filming *Star Wars* and Bill Clinton on a visit to Sydney.

Celeb Scoop: Susan spent four days searching for the perfect real Christmas tree for Nicole Kidman and Tom Cruise. Reportedly, Susan also did the flowers for Nicole's wedding to Keith Urban in 2006. Susan was also used by Sir Paul McCartney and his wife Linda to decorate their rental house in Cremorne when they visited Australia a decade ago with their daughter Stella.

The Inner West

'It's always great to come home and feel support from the people and feel that recognition of what's happened. It was Erskineville Kings *that I think today got me two roles directly.'* Hugh Jackman, actor

If you want pretension, glamour, people-watching and over-the-top establishments, you won't find them in Sydney's inner west. Comprised of waterside suburbs such as **Balmain** and **Drummoyne**; arty hubs like **Glebe**, **Newtown** and **Erskineville**; and multicultural meccas like **Leichhardt**, **Marrickville** and **Haberfield**, the suburbs which make up the city's inner west are as varied in their attractions as they are in their communities, but they all share the same laidback village vibe.

Forget your cocktail-sipping, stiletto-heeled, Street Tropez-tanned glamour crowd—inner west living is all about being low-key. Old-style pub and cafe cultures are stronger here than anywhere else in Sydney—visit Darling Street in Balmain, Enmore Road in Enmore, King Street in Newtown and Norton Street, Leichhardt—as is market shopping (Balmain and Glebe) and a lively music and theatre scene showcased in venues such as the Enmore Theatre and the Seymour Centre.

Cuisine in the inner west is impressive, though not because of its fine dining or silver-service restaurants. The west is famous for its authentic, home-style food and it's all about cultural diversity. Traditional style Asian, Thai, Japanese, Greek, Italian and more—even Indigenous—can all be found somewhere in the inner west. Leichhardt and Haberfield are particular highlights for serious foodies, especially if good Italian food is your thing.

There are many A-list connections with the inner west, starting back in the 1800s when Mary Reibey, a pioneering entrepreneur, lived in Newtown—she now features on the Australian $20 note. Balmain is also home to one of Australia's greatest swimmers, Dawn Fraser,

The Inner West

former Olympic medallist, who now has a pool named after her in the area.

Famous types who don't conform to the attention-seeking, party-obsessed stereotype regularly splashed about in the tabloids love the fact that they can live here and come and go as they please in relative anonymity.

Local stars Russell Crowe, Sam Worthington, Daniel Johns and Natalie Imbruglia have all been spotted enjoying the fuss-free existence of the area, and international rock chick Avril Lavigne stopped into Newtown's Vendor (229 King Street, Newtown) to buy a pair of sneakers.

Australian singer/songwriter Alex Lloyd, who grew up in Balmain and still lives in the area today, used to play at a Balmain pub when he was in his early teens. Without a car, he and his band had to get their gear to the pub in a shopping trolley! Another famous Balmain resident is actor Bryan Brown, who lives in a large heritage-listed terrace on Wharf Road with his family.

Lots of other Australian identities also currently live or have lived in one of the inner west areas—members of bands like The Whitlams, Frenzal Rhomb and Youth Group, actor Rose Byrne, boxer Jeff Fenech, broadcaster Alan Jones, musician Paul Mac, the Grammy Award-winning Wolfmother and Oscar-winner Judy Davis.

Many of our most famous entertainment exports also have close associations with various inner west areas, usually relating to work projects they have been involved with. *X-Men* star Hugh Jackman filmed *Erskineville Kings*, the movie that he believes gave him his Hollywood break, in the inner west, and *The Adventures of Priscilla, Queen of the Desert*, starring Guy Pearce and Hugo Weaving also used locations in the area.

Erskineville was also a backdrop for *The Matrix* and nearby Marrickville featured in *Strictly Ballroom*. The rooftop scene with Paul Mercurio—complete with Hills Hoist clothesline and Coca-Cola billboard—was filmed on top of the travel agency on the corner of Marrickville and Victoria Roads.

Away from the hustle and bustle of the city, areas of the inner west have been used as locations and design references for big-budget feature films. Balmain's White Bay Power Station was used for *The Matrix Reloaded* and *The Matrix Revolutions* (some subway scenes were also filmed at the Eveleigh Railyards in Redfern), and King Street Newtown was used as a backdrop in the Australian film *Candy* with Heath Ledger and Abbie Cornish. Most recently, Bollywood film-makers used the historic Street Stephen's Church in Newtown as a backdrop for the colourful Bollywood film, *Heyy Babyy*.

Homebush Bay, the HQ of Sydney's 2000 Olympic Games, sits on the furthest fringe of the city's inner west, but is a notable place of interest especially for sport-lovers. It was, after all, the home of 'the best Olympic Games ever'. Look out for Sydney Olympic Park's The Dome on the big screen, too, as it was used in the movie *Son of the Mask* starring Jim Carrey.

'*When I'm away from Sydney I miss the atmosphere. And the weather, the weather is pretty spot on—in summer it's pretty nice.*'
Alex Lloyd, singer/songwriter

Restaurants, bars & pubs

Canteen

332 Darling Street, Balmain
Phone: (02) 9818 1521
Grab yourself a coffee and an outside table, and watch the world go by.

Celeb Scoop: The fact that Canteen is owned by Aussie actor Steve Bisley (from TV shows like *Water Rats, Police Rescue, Frontline* and many more) means that you'll often find someone from the world of showbiz hanging out here. You might even find Bisley himself serving your food!

Lou Jacks

420 King Street, Newtown
Phone: (02) 9557 7147

The little courtyard out the back offers some solace from busy King Street and is a popular spot for brekkie because of its fried haloumi.

Celeb Scoop: Although unassuming, the cafe can boast of clientele like Natalie Imbruglia, members of Silverchair, and local identities such as Murray from children's group The Wiggles.

Bank Hotel

324 King Street, Newtown

Phone: (02) 8568 1900 ***Web:*** www.bankhotel.com.au

An extensive $5 million renovation has given this spot a new lease on life. Play a game of pool in the front bar, head upstairs to the spacious cocktail lounge, the Velvet Room, or grab a top-quality Thai meal from the restaurant. This isn't a grungey dive—it's definitely swish these days.

Celeb Scoop: Check the back room and other nooks and crannies for celebrities hiding out—actor Sam Worthington has enjoyed a few quiet drinks here in his time.

Rose of Australia Hotel

1 Swanson Street, Erskineville

Phone: (02) 9565 1441

Low-key and grungey, there's not a glimmer of pretention at The Rose so you won't find your glitzy, glam set here, but you just might spring an actor, muso or TV type. Frenzal Rhomb, Gia Carides and Nova 969's funny radio duo Merrick Watts and Tim Ross have all been to the Rose.

Celeb scoop: It was here that Aussie rocker Ian Moss from Cold Chisel jumped onstage on the spur of the moment and delivered an impromptu performance.

Erskineville Hotel

102 Erskineville Road, Erskineville

Phone: (02) 9565 1608

Down to earth and laid back, sports mad celebs like to come here to watch their teams on the big screen.

Celeb Scoop: Russell Crowe has been spotted here watching his favourite footy code, rugby league.

Imperial Hotel

35 Erksineville Road, Erskineville

Phone: (02) 9519 9899

Until the arrival of *Priscilla, Queen of the Desert*, Erskineville was a little short on landmarks. Thanks to the film's opening sequence, the classic Art Deco 'Impy' is now firmly in the world's mind, and this gay and lesbian hang out now has celebrity status in its own right.

Celeb Scoop: Hugh Jackman filmed many scenes here for *Erskineville Kings* in the downstairs area of the pub.

Norton Street, Leichhardt

Referred to as Sydney's 'Little Italy' because of its strong Italian community and its stretch of traditional style Italian restaurants and cafes, apart from the obvious—espressos, pasta and gelato—you can also pick up great Euro-inspired lifestyle and homeware pieces, take in a movie at Palace Cinemas or soak up the European atmosphere in the piazza of the Italian Forum. Every year there street is closed off for a day of festivities for the Norton Street Festival.

- **Palace Cinemas** 99 Norton Street
  Phone: (02) 9550 0122 *Web:* www.palacecinemas.com.au
- **Italian Forum** 21-23 Norton Street
  Phone: (02) 95180077 *Web:* www.italianforum.com.au
- **Bar Italia** 169 Norton Street
  Phone: (02) 9560 9981

Celeb Scoop: The premiere of *Love's Brother* was held at Palace Cinemas in 2004, with the film's stars Adam Garcia and Amelia Warner. It was also here that a young Rose Byrne did press here *for My Mother Frank* before she hit the big time. Aussie actor Alex Dimitriades tried to use his star power to convince the staff to re-open the kitchen at *Bar Italia* after it had closed for a late-night snack ... he was unsuccessful!

Theatre, cinema & music
Enmore Theatre

130 Enmore Road, Newtown

Phone: (02) 9550 3666 *Web:* www.enmoretheatre.com.au

One of the best performance spaces to see live music acts, this traditional theatre features two levels, and for bands that require it there's usually a dance floor area at the front for serious moshers. The atmosphere inside its walls is incredible—many big-name bands have unleashed their sounds here including Placebo, Joss Stone and Ben Harper, and Aussie acts like Missy Higgins, Keith Urban, Jet, Eskimo Joe and Alex Lloyd. It has also played host to visiting and local-hero comedy acts. The original *Wogs out of Work* stage show, starring Nick Giannopolous, played at the Enmore for 16 months in the late 1980s.

Celeb Scoop: When actor Patrick Swayze was in Sydney staying at the Park Hyatt he asked hotel staff to take him to hear some Australian music. He ended up at the Enmore Theatre watching Midnight Oil and wearing a baseball cap and glasses, completely unnoticed from the wings of the theatre.

@Newtown RSL

52 Enmore Road, Newtown

Phone: (02) 9557 5044 *Web:* www.atnewtown.com.au

This popular local has lost its RSL feel after serious renovating. Now there's something going on every night of the week and it's a great place to pop in for free local live music or a game of Texas Hold Em Poker.

Shopping
Darling Street, Balmain

Shopping in Balmain is centred around the suburb's main strip: Darling Street. An eclectic fusion of bars, pubs, cafes, restaurants and boutiques selling jewellery, books, clothing, antiques and homewares, the weekly Balmain market is held in the grounds of St Andrews Congregational Church, while the Rozelle markets are held closer to Victoria Road on Saturdays and Sundays from 10 am to 4 pm.

- **Victoire** 258 Darling Street
  Phone: (02) 9818 5529
  This bakery is a must for bread-lovers.
- **Emile's Fruit & Vegetables**
  321 Darling Street
  Phone: (02) 9810 2759
  Web: www.emiles.com.au
  Delights for the carb-conscious.
- **Belle Fleur Fine Chocolates**
  658 Darling Street
  Phone: (02) 9810 2690
  Web: www.bellefleur.com.au
  Sweet tooths will be sorry if they miss these carefully crafted chocolates, made daily and sold by weight.

Cerrone

13–19 Catherine Street, Leichhardt

Phone: (02) 9569 8500 **Web:** www.cerrone.com.au

It's hard to find a jeweller more connected to celebrity than Nicola Cerrone. Step inside his Leichhardt store and you will see caches of awards, and photographs of stars that wear his jewellery. Aussie fans include Delta Goodrem, Kate Fischer, Lady Sonia McMahon and Kerri-Anne Kennerley. Many sporting stars are also fans, like Dwight Yorke, former world champion boxer Kostya Tszyu and cricketer Ricky Ponting, who had Cerrone make an engagement ring for his wife. Tyra Banks, Janet Jackson and Diana Ross—who always wears Cerrone at her Sydney concerts—are fans.

Celeb Scoop: Cerrone sold an exquisite pink diamond to Barbra Streisand who later accused him of selling her a fake—an easy mistake to make as the diamond was flawless.

'I grew up in Balmain and there was a big group of us from the area who would catch the ferry over to the Rocks and take acting classes at the Australian Theatre for Young People.' **Rose Byrne, actor**

Planet Cake

106 Beattie Street, Balmain

Phone: (02) 9810 3843 **Web:** www.planetcake.com.au

Owner Paris Cutler has been baking special event wedding cakes for Sydney's society set and visiting celebrities for over a decade.

Celeb Scoop: Planet Cake created the large cream, tiered lacy wedding cake for Keith Urban and Nicole Kidman in 2006. Several other companies tried to take credit for the cake, but it was in this Balmain couture cake house that their cake was created.

Over The Bridge

'I lived in the Mosman area, in a beautiful place called Cremorne Point, which lies on the north side. Sydney is surrounded by water, and we were right there on the harbour. We didn't have a view of the Opera House or anything like that, because we were looking in the opposite direction. Nevertheless, it was a beautiful view.'
Naomi Watts, actor

The celeb sightings don't stop once you cross the Sydney Harbour Bridge, so don't be afraid that you'll be lost in a suburban hell if you leave the CBD.

First stop over the bridge, on the right-hand side, is the salubrious suburb of **Kirribilli**, home to the Prime Minister and Governor-General. Prime Minister John Howard is regularly seen taking an early-morning walk around the foreshore with his minders. Don't be fooled by the seemingly small Victorian terraces—the median price for a house in Kirribilli is more than $1 million. On the left-hand side as you cross the bridge is **Milsons Point**, home to the iconic Luna Park and the North Sydney Olympic Pool.

On the other side of Lavender Bay is **McMahon's Point**. Once you're there, make sure you have your walking shoes on, and head up Blues Point Road (there may be a bus you can catch if it is a weekday), and check out the little village of local shops and restaurants. One of Sydney's largest magazine publishing houses, Pacific Magazines, as well as several book publishers, are located here, so celebrities, models and high-flyers are often spotted in the area.

Legendary Australian artist Brett Whiteley lived around the corner in **Lavender Bay**, and grew up in the upper middle-class suburb of **Longueville**—as did Nicole Kidman and tennis player John Newcombe.

Over The Bridge

Nicole Kidman still has strong ties with Longueville, as her parents and sister, Antonia, all live in the adjacent suburb of **Greenwich**. Antonia's property on Greenwich Road is where Nicole held her hens' night party before her wedding to Keith Urban, and ordered in a private chef for a simple meal of yum cha.

Close by is **Woolwich**, another leafy harbourside suburb. Comedian and radio personality Tim Ross (one half of the Merrick and Rosso radio team), and radio star/*Australian Idol* judge Kyle Sandilands call the area home. Drop in to the Woolwich Pier Hotel for fantastic views, and to spot the stars.

Cate Blanchett now is a full-time resident in her $10.2 million, 4,000-square metre property, 'Bulwarra', with her husband and children in nearby **Hunters Hill**. Purchased in 2004, mid 2007 the Oscar winning actress splashed out $1.5 million to transform the grand 1877 North Shore mansion into the ultimate eco-home. A 20,000 litre water tank, high tech solar panelling, low energy lighting and grey water recycling are among some of the features her home was installed with.

St Leonards, a fairly nondescript suburb, is frequented by stars visiting the Royal North Shore Hospital. Paris Hilton and Nicole Kidman have both visited ill children here. Russell Crowe's wife Danielle Spencer gave birth to the couple's two sons here, as did Lleyton Hewitt's wife, Bec.

The further north-west you go, the bigger the properties get, some sprawling out over dozens of acres. A farm in the **Castle Hill** area has been used to film scenes for *Home and Away*. Nearby is **Hornsby**, where Mel Gibson hung out as a kid because it wasn't far from his school, St Leo's College, run by the Christian Brothers.

The best way to view the lower harbour suburbs is from the water. Ferries leave from Circular Quay and are an excellent way to get to Taronga Park Zoo at **Bradleys Head**—a guaranteed stop-over for international celebrities to admire cute Aussie animals. Bradleys Head also had an influx in celebrities in 2000 when it was part of the set of Tom Cruise's *Mission: Impossible II*.

The zoo is situated in **Mosman**, a genteel suburb with huge houses, big gardens and water views. Past and present Australian rugby union players John Eales, George Gregan and Phil Kearns, tennis ace Pat Rafter, actor Eric Bana and Australian artist Ken Done have all called Mosman home at one time or another. Properties on Kirkeswold Avenue and Burren Avenue start at around $12 million and go all the way up to $20 million.

When the rich and famous aren't sunning themselves on Mosman's quiet harbour beach **Balmoral**, they're shopping along Military Road, visiting cafes, designer boutiques and gourmet food stores. **Cremorne** is a five-minute drive away and was home to Naomi Watts before she moved to the US in the 1990s. Sir Paul and the late Linda McCartney rented a house in Cremorne in the 1990s. Decorated by Susan Avery (see index) with Tuberose and Lincoln red roses, all animal products and leather furniture was removed for their arrival to conform with the strict animal-friendly approach to life.

Over the Spit Bridge, **Manly** is known worldwide for its Norfolk Pine-lined beach. Watch the surfers, take a dip, get stuck into some classic fish and chips or try a fine-dining restaurant—and you might spot a celeb or two while you're at it. Nicole Kidman made one of her earliest acting debuts in Manly—her film *BMX Bandits* features a scene shot at the Manly Waterworks. Further north you'll find the long, lazy stretch of **Curl Curl Beach** (the Beach Kiosk at the southern end is a fave of world-champ surfer Layne Beachley) and even further north is **Dee Why**, another fantastic beach location.

Hotels
The Sebel Manly Beach

8–13 South Steyne, Manly

Phone: (02) 9977 8866 ***Web:*** www.mirvachotels.com.au/NSW
Refurbished in 2006, the Sebel Manly Beach encapsulates the relaxed
feel of Manly, with casually furnished rooms in natural seaside colours.

Celeb Scoop: The hotel was a hive of activity during the wedding of
Nicole Kidman and Keith Urban, when many of the couple's friends
and relatives chose to stay at the Sebel and enjoy the ocean views.

Restaurants, bars & pubs
Garfish

2/21 Broughton Street, Kirribilli

Phone: (02) 9922 4322 ***Web:*** www.garfish.com.au
This is a gorgeous, Landini-designed local restaurant with five
different fresh fish listed every day, and a range of sauces and
accompaniments. Casual, but great food, in a lovely leafy street.

Celeb Scoop: Ralph Fiennes is a fan of the fresh fish at Garfish
and was seen dining here just before he took the infamous flight to
India where he had a 'mile high' encounter with airline hostess Lisa
Robertson.

Aqua Dining

Olympic Drive, Milsons Point

Phone: (02) 9964 9998 ***Web:*** www.aquadining.com.au
The unique complex attached to the North Sydney Olympic Pool
includes this five-star restaurant with a view of the Art Deco 50-metre
swimming pool, as well as the harbour and the towering Harbour Bridge.

Celeb Scoop: Fans of the award-winning modern Australian
dishes include Megan Gale and TV personality Eddie McGuire.

Ripples Cafe

Cnr Paul and Northcliff Sts, Milsons Point

Phone: (02) 9929 7722 **Web:** www.ripplescafe.com.au

The sister restaurant to Aqua Dining, Ripples is a lower-key, outdoor cafe on the harbourfront, on the other side of the Olympic pool. It doesn't take bookings, but offers great, well-priced meals.

Milsons

17 Willoughby Street, Milsons Point

Phone: (02) 9955 7075

A real favourite of north-shore residents, Milsons serves fresh Australian food, showcasing Australian produce. Pre-theatregoers attending a performance at the Ensemble Theatre are frequent diners, along with appreciative locals.

Nu's Restaurant

178 Blues Point Road, McMahons Point

Phone: (02) 9954 1780

The north shore is not renowned for great restaurants, but Nu's is an exception. Named after the owner/chef and former Thai kickboxer, Nu Suandokmai, the diverse menu features Thai dishes with a French twist served in an old two-storey building with crystal chandeliers, ornamental fireplaces and slick white interiors. If celebs do cross the Bridge for a meal, this is often their first choice to stop.

Woolwich Pier Hotel

2 Gale Street, Woolwich

Phone: (02) 9817 2204 **Web:** www.woolwichpierhotel.com.au

This pub, originally built in 1885 but newly renovated, attracts wealthy local residents with the lure of its wraparound balcony and stunning harbour views. The bistro serves delicious meals including wagyu beef.

The Cabana Bar and Lounge

80 Christie Street, St Leonards

Phone: (02) 9436 4288 *Web:* www.cabanabar.com.au

Cabana Bar and Lounge used to be a rugby club but its tasteful refurbishment has meant that it has become one of the hottest places to drink on the lower north shore. It still gets a fair share of rugby players popping by, including John O'Neill, CEO of NSW Rugby Union, and ex-Wallabies, but also Australian TV and radio presenters like David Koch and Sami Lukis. They regularly have the best DJs in Oz playing, like Sneaky Sound System, The Bangang djs, Kid Kenobe, Shoreshock and MC Seany B.

Village Green Cafe

9/3 Mandalong Road, Mosman

Phone: (02) 9960 3448

Stop here to recharge with a coffee and yummy cake and you could be sitting next to stars such as Judy Davis, Colin Friels or Aussie artist Ken Done.

Bathers Pavilion Restaurant and Cafe

67 The Esplanade, Balmoral

Phone: (02) 9969 5050 *Web:* www.batherspavilion.com.au

This understated restaurant is a favourite with visiting celebrities due to inviting views and great food.

Will & Toby's

8-13 South Steyne, Manly

Phone: (02) 9977 5944 *Web:* www.willandtobys.com.au

Stylish but still relaxed, this beachside cafe-cum-restaurant is open seven days a week and is a great spot to grab a meal any time of day.

Celeb Scoop: Actor Melissa George is often seen dining here with a posse of Aussie celebrity friends.

Manly Wharf Hotel

East Esplanade, Manly

Phone: (02) 9977 1266 *Web:* www.manlywharfhotel.com.au

Step off the ferry and into the Jetty Bar and you'll be as close as possible to the water while keeping dry. This is a great Sydney pub.

Manly Ocean Beach House

Ocean Promenade, North Steyne, Manly

Phone: (02) 9977 0566

This casual restaurant with gourmet Australian food typifies Sydney in many ways—casual vibe meets sublime food and beautiful sea views. The ocean stretches out in front with a neat lawn meeting the sand and sea. Wooden floorboards complement white tablecloths.

Le Kiosk

1 Marine Pde, Shelly Beach

Phone: (02) 9977 4122 *Web:* www.lekiosk.com.au

This longstanding, beautiful beachside restaurant is a favourite among north shore residents. The beach is also a winner for families and those who baulk at crashing waves—it's in a sheltered nook, with plenty of shady trees and calm water. Le Kiosk has a delightfully rustic feel, with an open fireplace and extensive seafood menu.

Celeb Scoop: According to local folklore, Nicole Kidman checked out Le Kiosk as a possible venue for her wedding to Keith Urban, but had to pass it up due to security issues. However, it was the perfect backdrop for slalom skiing champion Zali Steggall and Olympic rower David Cameron's wedding.

Beach Kiosk

Carrington Pde, South Curl Curl
Phone: (02) 9907 2577

An unbeatable location, right on the water, this laidback kiosk is the perfect place to sit and watch the waves roll in and sample the delicious 'beach' food, like gourmet steak sandwiches, or the Curly Roll which comes highly commended by Layne Beachley.

'*My favourite spot is this place in Curl Curl and they do this amazing delicacy called the Curly Roll. It's a Turkish-type bread with a sweet chilli sauce, caramelised onions and fried eggs and bacon. It's my secret spot.*' **Layne Beachley, world-champion surfer**

Bacino Bar

18 The Strand, Dee Why
Phone: (02) 9982 1988

If you're looking for a scrumptious brekkie to start the day, head to this outdoor, beachside cafe.

Celeb Scoop: Laurence Fishburne enjoyed a full breakfast here of Italian scrambled eggs with prosciutto, tomato, basil and hollandaise sauce with woodfired toast when he was in town.

'*I love the upfrontness and honesty of Australians and the clear skies and greenness of the northern beaches suburbs.*' **Tom Cruise, actor**

Outdoor & adventure
Luna Park

1 Olympic Drive, Milsons Point

Phone: (02) 9033 7676 *Web:* www.lunaparksydney.com

It's hard to miss the huge face with big teeth and long eyelashes under the Harbour Bridge. The Sydney fun-park icon first opened in 1935 and was constructed in just over three months. It has been dogged with complaints from local residents, who dislike being interrupted by the carnival sounds and screams, but despite being closed several times, it's now open again and entry is free. Luna Park has a variety of stages, including the Big Top, where bands such as Nine Inch Nails, NOFX and Boys II Men have wowed crowds. And it has hosted some top gigs, including the MTV Australia Video Music Awards.

> Celeb Scoop: Anna Nicole Smith caused a stir at the MTV Awards in 2005 when she went onstage to present an award and pulled down her dress to reveal her breasts—with pink MTV stickers on her nipples!

Taronga Zoo

Bradleys Head Road, Mosman

Phone: (02) 9969 2777 *Web:* www.zoo.nsw.gov.au

Zoo's aren't usually renowned for their views but this is a great vantage point for Sydney. Its fabulous location means that just about every celeb has visited. Lleyton Hewitt and his wife Bec chose to hold their wedding reception here in September 2006. Once inside you can work your way down the hill. Packed with local flora and fauna, there's as much here for adults as children. See if you can spot Spike, the echidna that gets snapped and petted by all the international celebs. In fact, when Prince Harry was in town, he got to cuddle up to Spike, but thought the little fella was a porcupine!

'*When I was in Australia I went to [Taronga] zoo and they let me feed all the animals, but the zoo keepers wouldn't let me feed the zebras. They're pretty mean, apparently. There were lions and tigers, but they were like, 'Stay away from the zebras*'. **Frankie Muniz, actor**

Manly Beach

Whether you feel like swimming, surfing, paddling or just watching the beach crowd do their thing, Manly's world-famous beach is the place to do it. By ferry, it takes roughly 30 minutes from Circular Quay to arrive at the Manly ferry terminal. From here, the beachside corso is a two-minute walk away.

If you are keen to give surfing a go, Manly is a great place to learn and you might even find yourself sharing a break with seven-time world champion surfer Layne Beachley, who grew up in Manly and was surfing from the tender age of four. Layne loves North Steyne, which is the name of the patch of sand and surf to the left if you're looking at the main beach. Look out for other fit types like ironmen and women, as they're often training on the beach or in the water.

Manly was traditionally earlier to bed than the city (as was most of the north shore), but that is slowly changing with an influx of new hotels, restaurants and bars and a younger crowd inhabiting its swanky new apartment buildings. Apart from the beach, check out the local shops for trendy clothing from up-and-coming designers. The boys behind the celebrity fashion fave Tsubi/Ksubi and Jamie Blakey of One Teaspoon all grew up in Manly and regularly come back to the beach for design inspiration or for a surfing session.

'I grew up in the competitive environment of Manly beach, being a surfer and the only girl in the water. My favourite wave in Australia is Angourie on the northern NSW coast. And then Queenscliff and North Steyne.' **Layne Beachley, world-champion surfer**

Also on The A-list
Cardinal Cerretti Memorial Chapel

St Patrick's Estate, Manly

Web: www.sydney.catholic.org.au/ceretti

In 2006, thousands of well-wishers lined the streets of Manly, hoping to catch a glimpse of Nicole Kidman on her wedding day to Aussie country crooner, Keith Urban. The onlookers cheered when Nicole opened the window of her cream Rolls Royce to say thank you to the crowds. The 230 or so guests included Hugh Jackman and his wife Deborra-Lee Furness, director Baz Luhrmann, Russell Crowe, Naomi Watts and media moguls the Murdoch family. At the reception guests were treated to a rendition of Peter Allen's 'Tenterfield Saddler' by Hugh Jackman. Singer and Crowded House frontman Neil Finn then sang 'Fall at Your Feet', before Urban serenaded Kidman with his love song 'Making Memories of Us'.

Avalon, Palm Beach & Whale Beach

'*A marvellous summer is spending time with friends at Palm Beach, eating at Beach Road Restaurant, swimming in the surf, walking to the lighthouse or sometimes catching a ferry from Pittwater up to the Hawkesbury.*' Collette Dinnigan, fashion designer

Follow the winding road through the northern beaches of Sydney—past Manly, Curl Curl and Dee Why—and you will be treated to spectacular views of some of the city's cleanest surf beaches. A mecca for celebrities, stars try to fly under the radar in the northern beaches, leaving their entourage behind in order to blend in with the low-key suburbs.

The equivalent of The Hamptons in New York, **Palm Beach** has been the playground of the rich and famous since the 1930s when visiting movie stars would retreat to the beach for a quiet weekend. These days stars from Nicole Kidman to Cate Blanchett, Laurence Olivier, Vivian Leigh, John Cleese, Ken Rosewall, Peter Allen, Viv Richards, Tom Keneally, Spike Milligan, Colleen McCulloch, Mel Blanc, Billy Connolly, Pamela Stephenson, David Bowie, the Duke of Edinburgh, the Duke and Duchess of York, Mick Jagger and film director Peter Weir hire houses over summer or stay in local accommodation to have a solid rest and enjoy the quintessential Australian lifestyle.

In Christmas 2004, Steven Segal hired three homes here side by side! Floral and event stylist Susan Avery (see index) was hired to fill the house with festive flowers and even buy presents for his children.

Australian movie star Bryan Brown and his wife Rachel Ward have had a home there for years, as has Australia's wealthiest family, the Packers. A three-bedroom home in Karloo Parade was the temporary home for singer Olivia Newton-John while she was holidaying with her

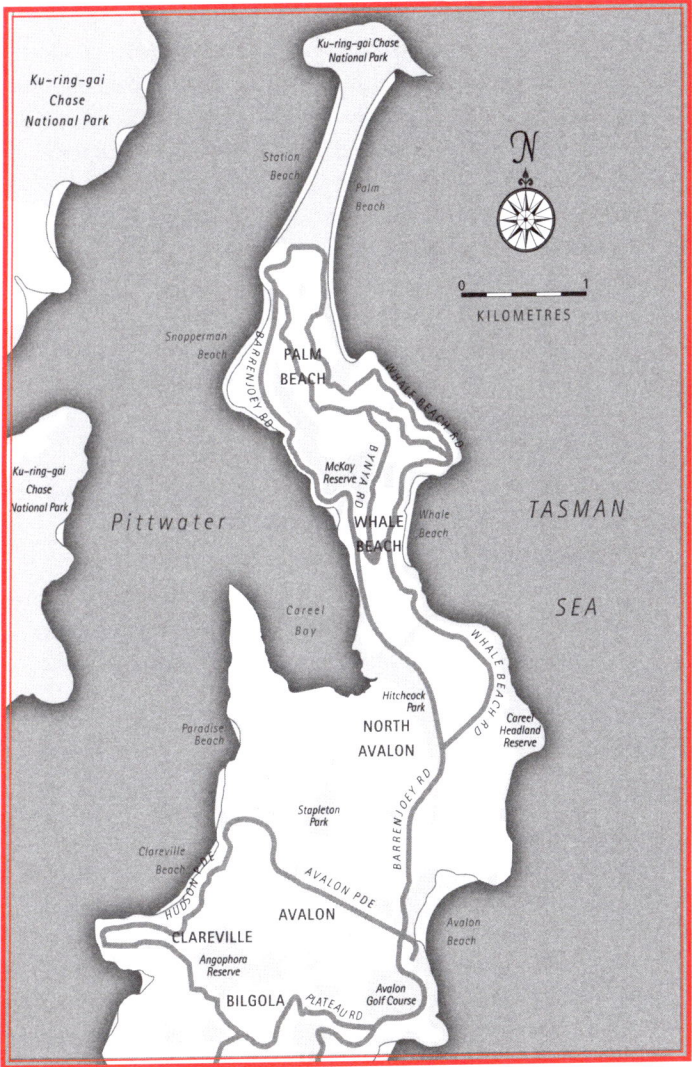

Avalon, Palm Beach & Whale Beach

daughter. Properties here are worth millions of dollars. The Rayner Road clifftop residence of Jigsaw clothing's Malcolm Webster, sold for $7 million not long ago. Prices of homes vary dramatically, but the starting price is around $2.5 million. Foreign visitors can be surprised at the lack of restaurants, shops and general facilities, but for locals, the lack of facilities is part of the charm. There are very strict planning and development laws preventing the place from becoming just another Australian beachside suburb packed with tourist shops.

Celebrities can also be seen in neighbouring **Avalon**. This is where surfing legend Kelly Slater had his Sydney base for 14 years before selling his apartment in 2007. It's also home to many of Australia's actors, scriptwriters, novelists and creative people. Actor and backyard renovation king Jamie Durie stays fit in Avalon.

The best place to spot the stars in Avalon is actually the pleasant shopping village, as nearly all celebrities must come here to fill up their pantries before moving on to **Palm Beach**, eight kilometres down the road.

Other than renting a house, the most glamorous place to stay in the area is Jonah's, situated in the suburb of Palm Beach. Rooms actually overlook Palm Beach's little sister, **Whale Beach**—another celebrity favourite and recognisable for its TV appearances as a backdrop on long running Australian soap, *Home and Away*.

Hotels
Jonah's

69 Bynya Road, Palm Beach

Phone: (02) 9974 5599 *Web:* www.jonahs.com.au
Jonah's is a glamorous European-style place to stay, which started off as a roadhouse in 1929, but today is complete with a five-star restaurant, regularly visited by the five-star crowd. Well-heeled Sydneysiders jet in by seaplane for lunch. Last renovated in November 2004, the rooms are pleasant, and most have a stunning out look across the sea from the hilltop. A celebrity favourite—expensive but beautiful.

Barrenjoey House

1108 Barrenjoey Road, Palm Beach

Phone: (02) 9974 4001 *Web:* www.barrenjoeyhouse.com.au

Situated above the Barrenjoey Restaurant, these boutique but more basic rooms (there are only seven) are well-priced, and most have water views. You might have to share a bathroom though!

Restaurants, bars & pubs

Barrenjoey Restaurant

1108 Barrenjoey Road, Palm Beach

Phone: (02) 9974 4001 *Web:* www.barrenjoeyhouse.com.au

This is a good, solid restaurant which seats over 100 and is packed on summer weekends.

The Beach House

227 Whale Beach Road, Whale Beach

Phone: (02) 9974 2727 *Web:* www.beachhouserest.com.au

The Beach House, just around the corner from the Barrenjoey Restaurant, seems to have ever changing chefs, but they present superb breakfasts, lunches and dinners, accompanied by great Australian wines.

Outdoor & adventure

Avalon Beach

Take a 45-minute drive from the CBD and you'll find yourself at Avalon, one of the city's stunning northern beaches. This is the beach *Baywatch* producers wanted to move filming of the hit American series to, but had their plans overruled by the Avalon community in the late 1990s. The beach itself is a beautiful curving surf beach, patrolled during summer by lifesavers from the Avalon Beach Surf Lifesaving Club.

'I like to do a bit of surfing and soft sand running on the northern beaches. Avalon is one of my favourites.' **Jamie Durie, TV personality**

Palm Beach

Huge houses, a beautiful stretch of sand and celebs aplenty are the drawcards of this beach. Australia's richest family, the Packers, own one of the best properties in Palm Beach, a mansion with a 40-metre beach frontage on Ocean Road, rumoured to be worth $30 million. Next door is Kalua, a gigantic property owned by enigmatic business identity Ian Joye. It's worth more than $10 million but for around $33,000 a week, stars can rent it out. Notable guests include British comedian and actor John Cleese, Elle Macpherson and Nicole Kidman.

Tennis ace Lleyton Hewitt and his wife Bec have a $4.5 million mansion here, heavily patrolled by security guards to prevent paparazzi shots. Local TV stars can be spotted most of the year, since for 18 years Palm Beach has been the backdrop for popular Aussie soap *Home and Away*. The Palm Beach Surf Club is used as the Summer Bay Surf Club. On the Pittwater side of the beach, you can have a coffee at the coffee shop often captured on the small screen. To catch them filming outdoor scenes, go to the South Palm Beach Rocks or Governor Phillip Park at North Palm Beach.

'There is nothing that beats the view of Palm Beach from the lookout at West Head or the view from the lookout at Bilgola Beach. Sydney is one of the best places to live.'
Bec Hewitt, actor

Out of Town

'I went wine-tasting in the Hunter Valley and stayed at this incredible place called the Tower Lodge.' **Kate Bosworth, actor**

If you don't mind a drive or a picturesque train ride, you can take a day or weekend trip to some great celeb hangouts just out of the city. The **Hunter Valley** is heaven for wine and food-lovers; the **Blue Mountains** are arty and full of natural beauty; the **South Coast** is a quiet stretch of towns with some gorgeous unspoilt little hideaways; and the **Hawkesbury River** area makes a great day trip for ordinary Sydneysiders and camera-weary famous folks alike.

Hunter Valley

170 kilometres (two hours drive) north west of Sydney

Web: www.huntertourism.com

Riding in a horse-drawn carriage through Australian vineyards has to be the best way to travel to dinner, and that's just one of the experiences on offer in the Hunter, a wine area frequently visited by visiting celebrities from golfer Greg Norman to chef Jamie Oliver. The girl being dubbed as 'the new Nicole Kidman' and allegedly responsible for the break-up of Ryan Phillipe and Reese Witherspoon, Abbie Cornish, grew up here, along with Aussie rugby star Andrew Johns and his brother Matthew, in nearby Cessnock.

World-class wineries sit next to art galleries, restaurants, lodges and hotels. You can get around on minibuses or even by bike, and wine-tasting here won't cost you a cent. Tempus Two is one of the stand-out wineries, established by local personality Lisa McGuigan. INXS performed on their second Aussie tour here with new lead singer, JD Fortune, supported by Scottish band, Simple Minds.

There is accommodation from one end of the scale to the other in the area—just take your pick. Entertainment-wise, there's plenty on offer

The wineries host regular outdoor concerts in summer, with operas, pop concerts and jazz are performed live. Huge names have been centrestage here—Diana Ross, Elvis Costello, Harry Connick Jnr and Tom Jones— along with many of Australia's great musicians and operatic stars.

Try a round of golf at The Vintage Golf Club, designed by golf pro Greg Norman who is world renowned for desiging challenging and visually stunning courses. Celebrities who've made their way from Sydney to play The Vintage include Steve and Mark Waugh, Doug Walters, Kerri-Anne Kennerley, Sami Lukis, Tim Webster, John Newcombe, Peter Sterling, Paul Vautin, Duncan Armstrong, Mark Ella and Andrew Johns.

Hotels

Tower Lodge, Halls Road, Pokolbin
Phone: (02) 4998 7022 *Web:* www.towerlodge.com.au
Tower Lodge has the crown as the best place to stay. Opened in 2000, the service, home style lodge and room decor is heavenly.

Peppers Convent, Halls Road, Pokolbin
Phone: (02) 4998 7764 *Web:* www.peppers.com.au/Convent
A stately manor house set right in the vineyards. Stay in a room with high ceilings and a gorgeous outdoor terrace for summer breakfasts.

Restaurants, bars & pubs

Roberts at Pepper Tree, Halls Road, Pokolbin
Phone: (02) 4998 7330 *Web:* www.robertsrestaurant.com.
This is the classic Hunter Valley restaurant. The setting in a small timber cottage sets the scene for a superb romantic meal.

Leaves and Fishes, 737 Lovedale Road, Lovedale
Phone: (02) 4930 7400 *Web:* www.leavesandfishes.com
This lunch spot could have been plucked straight off a Greek island.

The Blue Mountains
Katoomba, Leura & Blackheath

110 kilometres west of Sydney

Web: www.visitbluemountains.com.au

The Blue Mountains have a charm and class all of their own. The only son of Maharana of Mewar, owner of Lake Palace of Udaipur in India, and heir to the dynasty, Maharaj Kumar Sahib Lakshyaraj Singhji Mewar of Udaipur, spent three years at the Blue Mountains Hotel School.

Hotels
Lilianfels

Lilianfels Ave, Echo Point, Katoomba

Phone: (02) 4780 1200 *Web:* www.lilianfels.com.au

A Blue Mountains classic, with high tea and 85 boutique guest rooms. Darley's restaurant is steeped in history as it was the original homestead of Sir Frederick Darley, the sixth Chief Justice of New South Wales.

Mercure Grand Hydro Majestic

Great Western Highway, Medlow Bath

Phone: (02) 4788 1002 *Web:* www.hydromajestic.com.au

The most famous hotel in the mountains, with stunning views, a great spa and delectable high teas.

Restaurants, bars & pubs

· **Silk's Brasserie** 128 The Mall, Leura

Phone: (02) 4784 2534 *Web:* www.silksleura.com

This award-winning restaurant serves excellent, elegant country food.

Shopping

· **Leura Mall**

A great place to shop with fabulous restaurants and antique shops.

South Coast

180 kilometres from Sydney

Web: www.southcoast.com.au

Get away from the hustle and bustle and head down the coast. You won't know where to stop first, there's so much to see and do. Driving south out of Sydney, there are some gorgeous towns to stop off at including Berry, and Milton. A Devonshire tea with scones is a must—try the Pigeon House Tearooms (24 Clyde Ridge Road, Milton) and stop in for wine tasting at the Murramarang Vineyard (226 Bawley Point Road, Bawley Point.).

Hotels

· **Bannisters Point Lodge** 191 Mitchell Pde, Mollymook

Phone: (02) 4455 3044 *Web:* www.bannisterspointlodge.com.au

Bannisters Point Lodge is the highlight in the area in terms of accommodation, and plenty of celebrities have already discovered it. About 2.5 hours out of Sydney, the Lodge is in fact an old motel which has been completely revamped. Many celebs have stayed in the penthouse—a spacious room with flawless ocean views including 2DayFM's Kate Mac and her husband on their pre-honeymoon. Fashion designer Colette Dinnigan is a regular. A spa is on offer and the restaurant has sensational modern food.

Shopping

· **Peppergreen Antiques** Market Place, Old Hume Hwy, Berrima

Phone: (02) 4877 1488

Don't miss Peppergreen Antiques on the old Hume Highway in Berrima—it's not on the coast, but it's on the way down! This is mecca for antique needlework enthusiasts—a little slice of haberdashery heaven. Fashion designers such as Collette Dinnigan, Leona Edmiston and Lisa Ho are regular visitors, sorting through the antique buttons and fragments of lace for inspiration.

The Hawkesbury

100 kilometres from the city

Web: www.hawkesburyweb.com.au

The Hawkesbury River is one of New South Wales' magnificent natural features—the natural beauty of the area is the star attraction.

Hotels

· **Oxley Boatshed** Bar Point, Hawkesbury River

Phone: (02) 9985 9222

Accessible by boat or seaplane, the Oxley Boatshed encapsulates the rustic charm of a French farmhouse with the feel of an old beach house. It accommodates up to six people.

Restaurants, bars and pubs

· **Riverside Brooklyn Restaurant**

Level 1, Hawkesbury River Marina, Brooklyn

Phone: (02) 9985 7248 *Web:* www.riversidebrooklyn.com.au

The Riverside Brooklyn Restaurant is as casual as you'll get, with a large balcony. Oysters are supplied from a local oyster farm, and the seafood on the menu is abundant.

· **Peats Bite** Sunny Corner, Hawkesbury River

Phone: (02) 9985 9040 *Web:* www.peatsbite.com

Accessed by water or air only, Peats Bite is a tranquil, romantic spot to spend an afternoon. The modern Australian menu is diverse, with red meat dishes as well as seafood and chicken meals, and extensive desserts.

· **Cottage Point Inn** 2 Anderson Place, Cottage Point

Phone: (02) 9456 1011 *Web:* www.cottagepointinn.com.au

The Inn was originally the Cottage Point boatshed and general store. The building was converted to a restaurant in the 1970s and has been operating since. Fly there and back with www.sydneybyseaplane.com.au.

INDEX

205

shopping

theatre, cinema & music

First published in Australia in 2007 by
New Holland Publishers (Australia) Pty Ltd
Sydney • Auckland • London • Cape Town

1/66 Gibbes Street Chatswood NSW 2067 Australia
218 Lake Road Northcote Auckland New Zealand
86 Edgware Road London W2 2EA United Kingdom
80 McKenzie Street Cape Town 8001 South Africa

National Library of Australia Cataloguing-in-Publication Data:

Leith-Manos, Renae.
        The red carpet guide to Sydney : the essential guide to
        Sydney's celebrity hotspots.

        Includes index.
        ISBN 9781741105407 (pbk.).

        1. Celebrities - Homes and haunts - Guidebooks. 2. Sydney
        (N.S.W.) - Guidebooks. I. Title.

        919.44

Publisher: Fiona Schultz
Designer: Tania Gomes
Researchers: Harriet Farkash, Rochelle Cave, Laura Parker
Production Manager: Linda Bottari
Printer: Ligare Book Printers, Sydney New South Wales
Cover photograph: Getty Images and New Holland Image Library

10 9 8 7 6 5 4 3 2 1